29Grandpa, tell us about

Phi

Exploring the Amazing Golden Ratio

By John P. Choisser

ISBN 978-1719939195

Published by Readerplace Books, LLC

www.readerplace.com

San Diego, California, USA

Dedication

To Susan and Doc

Susan, my daughter who blessed the world with the three children who are the stars of this book.

And to Doc

It seems kind of strange to dedicate a book to someone you know so little about.

When I was a little kid, we lived near Williams Field, later named Williams Air Force Base, near Chandler, Arizona. It was near the end of WWII, and we and our neighbors would often rent a room to someone from the base. I suppose the base couldn't grow fast enough, because there were always base personnel (both army and civilian) walking through the neighborhoods looking for a place to stay. We made many life-long friends that way, some of whom actually came back to Arizona after they got out of the service. I suppose Doc was renting a room from us, or from one of our neighbors.

During the hot desert evenings, we would sit in our glider in the front yard making a breeze by swinging back and forth. Doc would join us, and tell us about the heat lightning on the horizon, or about meteors, or ball lightning, thunderstorms and earthquakes, or, one special night, a lunar eclipse! I was fascinated.

We talked about astronomy, geology, electricity, foreign lands, and other things that gave me amazement and lots to think about. No wonder I became an engineer!

Decades later, going through Mom's stuff, I found a photograph of a little switch engine hanging in the air being unloaded with a crane from a railroad flat car. On the back of the photo, Mom had written "Doc's engine". I don't know where his knowledge of science and technology came from, but during the War he drove a switch engine on the base!

So, Doc, whoever you were, whatever your name is, and wherever you are, thank you. I hope that I can show a few other kids out there how wondrous our universe is, the way you did for me.

Preface

This is a book for people from 9 to 90 who like surprises. And beauty. My intention is to show the beauty in both nature and mathematics, with some surprising connections that will make you stop and think. With this and future books, I want to foster curiosity, particularly in young people who might now see beyond boring or dull school subjects into a new world of science, physics, engineering, and math.

In this book, Grandpa and his grandchildren embark on an adventure into the fascinating connection between nature and a number called phi (ϕ). Phi is also called the Golden Number, the Golden Ratio, the Golden Section, and the Divine Proportion. It is an irrational number, like pi (π), and its value is approximately 1.618.

One of the interesting facts about phi is its relationship to the famous Fibonacci series and to the beautiful logarithmic spiral, one of the most beautiful shapes in nature. Grandpa and the children find Fibonacci numbers in the numbers of flower petals, the number of spirals on pinecones and pineapples, the shape of seashells, the genealogy of bees, how falcons attack their prey, the shape of soccer balls, and more. From the structure of a carbon crystal, to the spiral one sees in distant galaxies, phi is pervasive throughout nature. And over recorded history, it has had an effect on science, religion, astronomy, mathematics, art, and architecture.

I hope that this book results in a few young people realizing that the wonders of nature and mathematics are worth more exploration, and that because of that, our society gains a few good engineers, physicists, and natural scientists.

John P. Choisser

San Diego, California

Table of Contents

List of Figures

13

Introduction

This is the first of a series of "Grandpa" books, intended to surprise, fascinate, and amaze young people (of any age!) with the wonders of science and nature. This book is about phi, the mysterious and almost magic number that connects nature and mathematics.

Phi has been known and marveled at for centuries, and has attracted the attention of mathematicians, physicists, naturalists, artists, architects, and even spiritualists over the years. In this book, we will explore, through the eyes of Grandpa's grandchildren, this number, known variously as the Golden Number, the Golden Ratio, and the Divine Proportion, among others. Our Reader will be given chances to participate, so that anyone of any age might experience for themselves the surprises we find.

Yes, surprise is the word. Surprise is the basis for good jokes, mystery stories, and unexpected pleasurable experiences. Math is dull, science is boring. Maybe that's true in the classroom, but not with Grandpa!

Chapter 1. Phi, the Golden Ratio

"Grandpa", Courtney said, "tell us about the Golden Ratio".

Grandpa had just read a short article about this a week earlier, and it had reminded him how fascinated he had been when he had first discovered this magical link between mathematics and nature. It all begins with a simple concept, and develops into complex relationships that have intrigued and puzzled people for centuries.

Three grandchildren, Courtney, 14, Hunter, 11, and Morgan, 8 were over for the weekend, and everyone had been having a wonderful time swimming, barbequing, and enjoying the balmy summer weather. So it was time for a rest, and their ears perked up when Grandpa gave them a preview of the things they could explore.

"OK", Grandpa said, "what do you think is the link between a sea shell and a bee's grandparents? Or the shape of a distant galaxy and raising rabbits? Or the kitties running up the stairs and a pineapple? Or a pinecone and a sunflower? Or how leaves are arranged on a plant's stem? Or seeds in an apple core?"

"Huh?" "You're kidding". "Is this a joke?"

"Nope", Grandpa replied, "it's real. And I think you will discover some very entertaining and amazing things as we explore this subject", Grandpa replied. "And since we are writing our adventures into a book, we are going to take our Readers along with us. We will even give our Readers some exercises that they can do on their own, along with web search ideas. Sound like fun?"

"Where do we start", Hunter wondered. "At the beginning, I suppose, wherever that is."

Counting Things Outdoors

"Yep, you're right". Grandpa said, "We need to start by counting things. Let's start outside. Morgan, grab a pad and pencil – you're going to be the record keeper."

Everybody followed Grandpa out into the yard where he started looking at the plants and flowers. "Here," Grandpa said, "look at this flower."

Figure 1.1. Pink Hibiscus

"OK, how many petals?" Grandpa asked.

"Five."

"Right."

Figure 1.2. Vine Leaves

"Here the new leaves are growing in pairs," said Grandpa, "let's write down a two."

"Look over here, Grandpa," Hunter said, "Little stars, with five points."

Figure 1.3. Star Flowers

"Another five."

Figure 1.4. Yellow Flower

"Just count the top row on this one, even though there's a back row petal peeking through. How many?" asked Grandpa.

"Thirteen," replied Courtney.

"What numbers do we have so far, Morgan?" asked Grandpa.

"Two, five, and thirteen," he said.

"Let's find a three," Grandpa challenged.

"Boy, fives are everywhere, it seems," said Courtney.

"Here's a three," Morgan announced.

Figure 1.5. Clover Leaf

"Great. Now grab that pinecone over there and let's go back inside. Oh, and that orange flower with lots of petals. We might have to dissect that!" Grandpa said.

Figure 1.6. Orange Flower

Back inside, the kids started carefully taking apart the flower. When they finished, they had discovered that it had 21 petals.

Figure 1.7. Orange Flower Petal Count

"What are the numbers now," asked Grandpa.

"We've got 2, 3, 5, 13, and 21 so far," replied Morgan.

"Hmmm," Grandpa said, "we're missing number 8."

"What?" Courtney said.

"Let's look at the pinecone," Grandpa suggested. "Look at how its parts are arranged in spirals. Not only that, but there are spirals going in two directions. How can we count them without getting confused?"

"Well, we need to mark them somehow," replied Hunter.

"Here's some white correction fluid," said Morgan. "Let's try that."

So they carefully marked one row of each spiral direction, and could then count the rows.

Figure 1.8. Pine Cone

"Five one way and eight the other," announced Courtney. "There's your missing eight, Grandpa. Why was there supposed to be an eight?"

"You'll see," replied Grandpa with a wink.

Counting Things in the Kitchen

"Let's see what we've got here," Grandpa said. "We have a pineapple, an apple, and a tomato. First, what do you notice about the pineapple?"

"The outside looks a lot like a pinecone, with spirals," Courtney said.

"Right," Grandpa replied. "Why don't you mark the spirals like we did the pinecone, and the boys and I will look at some of the other stuff."

"Here's a Roma tomato, Hunter. Whack it in half."

Figure 1.9. Roma Tomato

"Two sections," reported Hunter. "That's another 2."

"Morgan, how many bumps are there on the bottom of that Delicious apple?"

"Five."

"Let's cut that in half," said Grandpa.

Figure 1.10. Apple Sections

"Five sections inside", said Morgan.

"The five bumps are peculiar to the Delicious variety of apple, but the five sections inside are very common," said Grandpa. "You and the Reader should search Google Images for 'apple section' some time, and you'll see what I mean."

Cutting the banana in half showed that it also had five seeds arranged in five internal sections.

"How are you doing with that pineapple," asked Grandpa.

"Done," replied Courtney.

Figure 1.11. Pineapple Spirals

"And the count?" asked Grandpa. "Drum roll, please."

"Eight and thirteen," replied Courtney. "I'm getting a little spooked by these numbers."

"By the way," said Grandpa, "what is the shape of each pineapple segment?"

"It looks like they all have five sides," replied Courtney.

"Yep, another 'five'. By the way, there is another set of spirals – five spirals. See if you can find them.

"Now, shall we review the list?" asked Grandpa.

"2, 3, 5, 8, 13, and 21," replied Morgan.

"Hey! Add two of them and you get the next number!" Hunter exclaimed.

"Another surprise!" Grandpa said. "Now it's time for a little history lesson.

"We've just discovered some numbers in nature that happen to be called Fibonacci numbers. They have an interesting connection between nature and mathematics, in case you haven't noticed. There is an important relationship between the Fibonacci number and phi, the Golden Number. Phi is also called other names, like the Golden Ratio, Golden Section, and even God's Number. You'll soon see why. But first, let's explore phi.

Chapter 2. Phi in Mathematics

Proportion

"The first thing we need to do is to understand proportion. Morgan, if you would be so kind as to bring that tablet over here, we'll do a little drawing".

"Now, things are in proportion if they keep the same look as they change their size. For example, the rectangles below are keeping the same proportions as they get bigger:"

Figure 2.1. Proportional Rectangles

"But these are not. They are getting bigger, but their proportions are changing. Do you see that?"

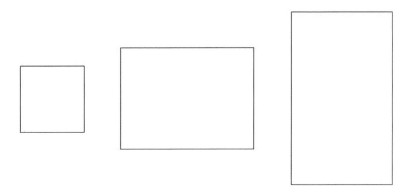

Figure 2.2. Non-Proportional Rectangles

"An everyday example of proportion is viewing something from different distances. It gets larger or smaller, but you can tell it's still the same shape."

Figure 2.3. Eiffel Tower Viewed from Different
Distances

"OK, Grandpa, I get the idea. But it doesn't work for people, does it? I mean, a baby doesn't look like a little adult, does it?"

"That's very true, Morgan. Your baby cousin Claire, at six months, like all babies, has a large head compared to her little body, but it's normal, because as we grow, the proportions change. Even though our heads get bigger as we grow, our arms and legs get bigger faster so our head looks smaller in proportion. So I think you guys have a pretty good grasp of proportion."

The Golden Ratio

"Now let's see how we can derive a very fundamental number having to do with proportion. And I want to point out that we are not the first to do this by a long shot. There is some historical evidence that people have known about and used this number for centuries. And its connection with nature is almost scary! You'll see why some people even call it God's Number."

"We're going to show the calculation of this number in the Appendix, and if you want to, we can go there now and show how we can derive it. But to save time, we can do that later, if you wish, and get on with the magic. Now here's the number:"

1.61803399...

Figure 2.4. The Golden Number Phi

"This number has been given the name phi or, in Greek, ϕ. The three dots following the number indicate that there are more digits to follow. In fact, there are an infinite number of digits following that never repeat themselves. This makes it an irrational number, which means that it can never be exactly expressed as a ratio, or fraction. By the way, the number .33333... also has an infinite number of digits, but it is a rational number because it can be exactly expressed as a fraction. What's the fraction?"

"1/3", replied Hunter.

"Right. Now, let's take turns with the calculator and play with this number a little. Reader, please get a calculator and join us!

Magic Math

Courtney, what is ϕ^2?

Well, 1.61803399 times 1.61803399 is …
What? Am I seeing things? It's 2.61803399!"

"Funny, huh? Same as 1 +ϕ. Now, Hunter, I
would like you to calculate 1/ϕ, so you will need to use
the reciprocal key on the calculator. Does it have one?"
Grandpa asked.

"It must be the key that is labeled 1/x. Right?"
he asked.

"Yep, that's the one. So enter 1.61803399 and
hit the reciprocal key."

"Oh, no, I get 0.61803399. What's with this
number, anyway? That's the same as ϕ-1!"

"Oh, wait!" Grandpa said, "That reminds me of
something. In Appendix A we will discover that there
were two solutions to our problem, one positive and one
negative. We forgot to calculate the negative solution.
What's that going to be, Courtney? Here's the equation
as a reminder:"

$$x = \frac{1 \pm \sqrt{5}}{2}$$

Figure 2.5. The Formula for Phi

"We'll use the minus sign instead of the plus sign. That, dear Grandpa, will be 1 minus 2.23606798 divided by two. Which is... I don't believe this. It's -0.61803399!

"Holy smoke!" Hunter exclaimed.

"I'm getting the creeps." Morgan said.

"And this is the only number in the world that behaves this way!" Grandpa added.

"Wait a minute", Morgan said, "What do the two solutions mean, plus1.618... and minus 0.618...?"

"You'll see that in the next section," teased Grandpa.

Finding Fibonacci

"Lot's more mysterious fun coming up," Grandpa promised. "To start the fun, I need a couple of numbers. Morgan, will you pick a number?"

"Well," he replied, "I'm eight. How's that?"

"Fine with me. How about you, Hunter?"

"If we're going to use ages, why not eleven for me?" he replied.

"OK, eight and eleven it is. Courtney, we are going to need to make a list of numbers, so grab that tablet, please. Oh, and we'll need a calculator again. Reader, get ready to join us!"

"I'm ready", Courtney said.

"Make a column of numbers, Courtney, and start with "8" and under it write "11". Now I want you to add the two numbers to get the third number, and then, from then on, get each new number by adding the previous two numbers. Let's see how that looks," Grandpa asked. "And let's invite our Reader to do the same thing."

Courtney started calculating: "Let's see, eight plus eleven is nineteen. Then eleven plus nineteen is thirty......"

In practically no time, Courtney had the following list:

8

11

19

30

41

49

79

128

207

335

542

877

1,419

2,296

3,715

6,011

9,726

15,737

25,463

41,200

66,663

Figure 2.6. A Recursive Series

"Now, Courtney," Grandpa said, "you can take a break from the calculator and let Morgan take over for a minute. The list is long enough now, and we are going to do something with it that will show a hidden surprise. I hope our Readers are doing this at home!

"By the way," Grandpa said, "this is called a recursive series, because each number is a function of the numbers that come before it; in this case adding the previous two numbers. There are other ways to generate a series. For example, an arithmetic series is generated by adding a number, say 'three' to each number. A geometric series might be generated by multiplying each number by five, for example, to get the next number. But this particular recursive series, where we add two numbers to get the next one, is special, which you'll see in a minute.

"Morgan, I would like you to divide the second number by the first number, please."

"OK, Grandpa, you mean 11 divided by 8? The answer is 1.375."

"Right. Hunter, would you do the next two", Grandpa asked.

"Sure, Grandpa. 19 divided by 11 is 1.7272727."

"Courtney, would you please do the next two?" Grandpa asked.

"30 divided by 19 is 1.5789473.", she replied.

"All right," Grandpa said, "let's take turns dividing and writing down the answer, and see where it leads."

11	÷	8	=	1.375
19	÷	11	=	1.7272727
30	÷	19	=	1.5789473
49	÷	30	=	1.6333333
79	÷	49	=	1.6122448
128	÷	79	=	1.6202531
207	÷	128	=	1.6171875
335	÷	207	=	1.6183574
542	÷	335	=	1.6179104
877	÷	542	=	1.6180811

Figure 2.7. Converging on Phi

"Whoa! What's going on here," Hunter exclaimed. "This number is changing less and less and it sure does look familiar."

"It's almost phi," added Courtney.

"Hmmm," Grandpa muttered, "let's keep going. Remember, phi to seven decimal places is 1.61803399.

1,419	÷	877	=	1.6180159
2,296	÷	1,419	=	1.6180408
3,715	÷	2,296	=	1.6180313
6,011	÷	3,715	=	1.6180349
9,726	÷	6,011	=	1.6180336
15,737	÷	9,726	=	1.6180341
25,463	÷	15,737	=	1.6180339
41,200	÷	25,463	=	1.618034
66,663	÷	41,200	=	1.6180339

Figure 2.8. Getting Closer to Phi

"So," Grandpa pronounced, "Morgan's and Hunter's ages lead us to the Golden Ratio. And this doesn't just appear to be so, it can be proven. Only you'll have to take my word on that for now."

"Only eleven and eight?" asked Hunter.

"No, any two numbers. That's why I said in the beginning I needed two numbers. Remember, it wasn't my idea to use your ages; you guys decided that. We could have started with any two, and even in reverse order! Try it yourself and see."

"Wow." said Morgan, "that's weird."

"I know," Grandpa replied, "and we're just onto something that has fascinated people for centuries. But first, let's take a dip and cool off. And here's where our Readers can do the same experiment with two numbers that they choose."

After a little fun and exercise, we took a rest, and we continued.

"Hey, Grandpa," said Morgan "you said this section was going to explain the + and − solutions to the Phi Equation."

"Right," replied Grandpa, "you can think about the two solutions as if you are proceeding up or down the list of numbers. For example, 5 times 1.618 gets you 8, which is the next number, and 8 times .618 gets you 5, which is the preceding number, if you round off the numbers."

Meeting Mr. Fibonacci

"People have known about the Golden Ratio for over two thousand years, and have noticed its presence in mathematics, art, and nature. We'll get to all of those things soon, but first I think it will be interesting to take a look at a man, who at a young age in the year 1202 (over eight hundred years ago!) fundamentally changed mathematics. And he also discovered the relationship with phi that we just experimented with.

"His name was Leonardo of Pisa, born in 1170. At that time, Pisa was a busy Italian seaport, and lots of goods were shipped and traded. The number system in use in Pisa at the time used Roman numerals. Now, I ask you, Courtney, if I have XXVI pounds of grapes, and you have MCXIV pounds, how much do we have together?"

"Ouch. That looks hopeless. There must be a way, though." Courtney replied.

"And that was only thinking about addition. You don't even want to consider multiplication. They certainly couldn't do math the way we do today, that's for sure," Grandpa continued. "They were very limited at math because they couldn't use their numbers, so they had to make calculations with an abacus. The abacus uses beads sliding on a set of wires that represent the quantities being computed. And you might also be interested to know that the abacus is still in use today in some parts of the world.

"In any case, when Leonardo was in his early thirties, his observations of the merchants and accountants had convinced him that the Roman numbering system needed to be changed to the Hindu-Arabic system of numbers we use today. He published a book that became very famous, even leading to a meeting with the Roman emperor Frederick II. And his "new math" became used very widely, as you can imagine.

"Today, Leonardo of Pisa is known as Fibonacci, which means son of the Bonacci family; a name that was given to him by a mathematician in the 1800's. Most people who recognize his name do so because of the mathematical series that is named after him. The Fibonacci Series is formed beginning with 1, which makes it the most fundamental of what we call an additive series, where each number is generated by adding the previous two numbers. Let's write down the Fibonacci Series:"

So with the help of Courtney, Hunter, Morgan, and the calculator, we began to generate the famous Fibonacci series.

"Wait a minute, Grandpa, one is only one number. How do we get started?" Morgan asked.

"Well," Grandpa said, "if there is no number before one, the next number must be one plus nothing, or one. What do you think of that?"

"Hmmm. I guess that's OK." Courtney conceded.

So we wrote:

1

1

2

3

5

8

13

21

34

55

89

144

233

377

610

987

1,597

50

2,584

4,181

6,765

10,946

17,711

Figure 2.9. The Fibonacci Series

"That should be plenty," Grandpa said. "Hunter, would you please divide 17,711 by 10,946 for us?"

"I knew it. It's 1.6180339."

"Yes," Grandpa said, "it's converging on phi, all right."

"I'm gonna freak out," said Morgan.

"You're usually freaked out," commented Courtney.

"Do you guys agree that there are an infinite number of Fibonacci numbers?" asked Grandpa.

"Well, I guess so," replied Courtney, "we could go on adding numbers together forever."

"If you had an infinite list of random numbers, would you think there would be the same number of odd and even numbers?" asked Grandpa.

"Sure," Hunter replied.

"OK, what about Fibonacci numbers? Take a look at the list," Grandpa suggested.

"Let's see," said Morgan, "The 'ones' are both odd, and then there's the 'two'. The next two, 'three' and 'five', are both odd, but the next one, 'eight', is even."

Courtney quickly scanned the list. Another surprise: there are two odd numbers followed by an even number.

"So," Grandpa announced, "there are twice as many odd numbers as even numbers in the series!"

Now comes a loaded question. "Are there more odd numbers than even numbers in the Fibonacci Series?"

"Sure," said Courtney. And the others nodded their agreement. "There are twice as many."

"Nope," Grandpa replied, "there are an infinite number of both odd and even numbers. The two infinites are the same, because for every odd number you list, I can list an even number, even though my list will contain larger and larger numbers than yours. It'll strain your brain, but that's the way infinity works!

"But if you throw in the irrational numbers in between the numbers in a list, like pi, phi, and e, you have a "larger" infinite set. Infinite sets are designated by the Hebrew letter *aleph* ($\aleph$), with aleph null ($\aleph_0$) and aleph one ($\aleph_1$) the names of the two sets I just mentioned. So you can have different "degrees of infinity", but even though in the Fibonacci series we have twice as many odd as even numbers, there are an equal (infinite) number of each of them. Now take an aspirin and lie down. That's what advanced math does – lots to think about!"

"Next we're going to tackle one of Fibonacci's most famous math problems. Raising rabbits!"

Raising Rabbits

After a swim and some snacks, we re-convened our little class.

"Next," Grandpa said, "we are going to look at one of the problems Fibonacci invented back in the year 1200. It's about raising rabbits."

"Rabbits? How did they get into this discussion?" wondered Hunter.

"That's part of the fun. Now here's the problem." Grandpa continued, "If I give you a pair of rabbits, and they have a pair of baby rabbits each month, and after a month each of the babies have babies, how many rabbits will you have at the end of the year?"

"Before long, the baby's babies will start having babies, and so on. Sounds like a lot of rabbits (and a hard problem to solve) to me." Courtney said.

"Well, the best way we can organize a problem like this is to make a chart. So let's go month by month. The first month, you only have one pair. At the end of the second month, they have a pair, and one pair per month after that. A month later, their babies have a pair, and so on. We'll draw two sizes of rabbits, so we can tell which pair are mature and which pair are babies.

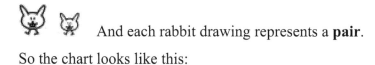 And each rabbit drawing represents a **pair**.

So the chart looks like this:

Figure 2.10. Raising Rabbits

"Grandpa," Courtney said, "your rabbits are very cute. But I'm confused about how the chart is made, and Morgan's eyes are glazing over."

"OK," Grandpa replied, "let's explain how the chart is made, look for a little magic in it, and take a break. At the end of month zero, I give you a pair of baby rabbits, shown in Row 0 by the baby rabbit symbol. By the end first month, your first pair matures, shown by the big rabbit in row 1 (or, as you would "address" the chart, in location 1A). So that's all you've got. But at the end of the second month, your first pair

55

have a pair of babies, shown at 2B. Does that make sense?"

"Sure," Morgan replied. "So we just take it step by step."

"Right on. At the end of the third month, we still have the original pair, at 3A, the original pair have had another set of babies, shown at 3B, and the baby pair in the second month (2B) have matured, shown in 3C. Courtney, would you like to tackle month 4?"

"Sure, Grandpa, let's see – we still have the original pair, at 4A, and they have had their monthly babies, shown at 4B. Last month's babies from 3B have matured, shown at 4C, we still have the pair from 3C, which we show at 4D. Plus, now we have 4D's new set of babies which we show at 4E. Whew!"

And we finished the chart up to row 7.

"Now, Morgan, how many mature pairs of rabbits do we have each month?" Grandpa asked.

"One the first month, one the second month, two the third month, three the next month, five the fifth month, eight the sixth month, and thirteen the seventh month."

Grandpa summarized: "So the numbers are 1, 1, 2, 3, 5, 8, and 13? Do these numbers look familiar?"

"Whoa," said Hunter, "it's the Fibonacci Series."

"Yes," Grandpa replied, "and how many baby pairs are born each month (not counting the original pair)?"

Courtney counted fast: "1, 1, 2, 3, 5, 8. There it is again!"

"And, Morgan, how many total rabbits are there each month?"

"1, 1, 2, 3, 5, 8, 13, and 21 the last month. There it is. All Fibonacci numbers again." he pondered. "I wonder why...."

"We'll get to that," Grandpa promised.

Chapter 3. Beautiful Spirals

The next weekend, Hunter was the first to bring up the curious things we had explored the week before. "Grandpa," he said, "We saw how phi and the Fibonacci Series are related to some pretty amazing things already. And you said there are lots more. What kinds of things do you mean?"

"Well," Grandpa replied, "let's take things in a manageable order. We'll start with geometry, and then you'll see how that leads to nature and growing things. How's that?"

"Great. Let's get started", said Courtney.

"One interesting way to start is to first draw what is known as the Golden Rectangle. You already know what a rectangle is; what do you suppose is special about the Golden Rectangle?"

"I'll bet phi is there," said Morgan.

"Correct. A Golden Rectangle has its sides in the ratio of 1 to 1.61803399... Here are two; one shown horizontally, and one shown vertically. If the short side is 1, the long side is phi."

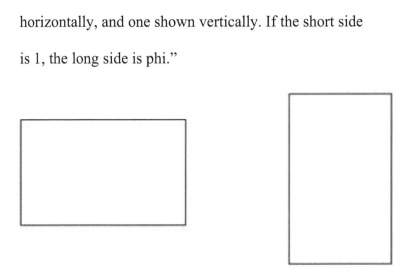

Figure 3.1. Golden Rectangles

Grandpa explained that the Golden Rectangle has been known for centuries, and is very famous among artists and architects. "Many people think that it is the most pleasing rectangle to the eye, and that it has therefore been used in the shape of everything from the Greek Pantheon to oriental vases. I'll show you some examples after a while," Grandpa promised. "You and our Readers can also do an Internet search on the Golden Ratio or Golden Rectangle later.

"One of the interesting things about the Golden Rectangle is that it can be geometrically constructed. Construction in geometry means that it can be drawn using only a compass and a straight edge, without having to measure any lengths."

"Now that would be handy," Courtney surmised, "because 1.61803399 is kind of hard to find on a ruler. But how can such an irrational figure be constructed? And is it complicated?"

"Amazingly easy," Grandpa replied. "We start with a square, and mark the midpoint of one side. The midpoint can also be found with a compass and straight edge; if you want, I can show you how to do that later. Anyhow, here's the square with the midpoint of one side marked with a dot:"

"Now we draw a line from the dot to one corner of the square."

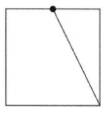

"And now we use that line as the radius for our compass and swing an arc up to meet the extension of the top line:"

"And the result is a Golden Rectangle!"

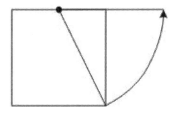

Figure 3.2. Construction of a Golden Rectangle

"Wow, that seems awfully easy for such an important irrational number," commented Hunter.

"That's part of its elegance," Grandpa replied. "But there are other examples; you can bisect a line, put the compass point on the center, draw a circle, and you have a circle and a diameter. What's that ratio?"

"Pi," said Courtney. "And it is also an irrational number: 3.14157..."

"OK," said Morgan, "but I'm sure we have more than just a rectangle here. And there must be more to it than just one that people think is pretty. And you're right, that seems like an awfully easy way to get a number as complicated as phi!"

"Yep", Grandpa replied, "that's a surprise, and it's only the beginning. Now let's take a larger Golden Rectangle:"

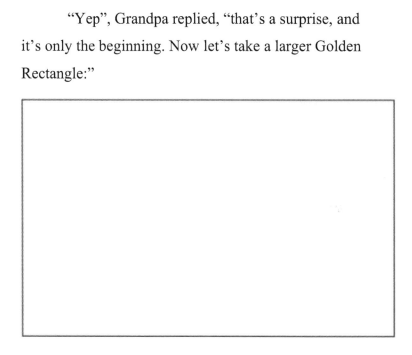

Figure 3.3. Dividing the Golden Rectangle 1

"Now if you will recall that when we constructed the Golden Rectangle, we started with a square. So if you think about it, if we whack off a square, we are left with another smaller Golden Rectangle:"

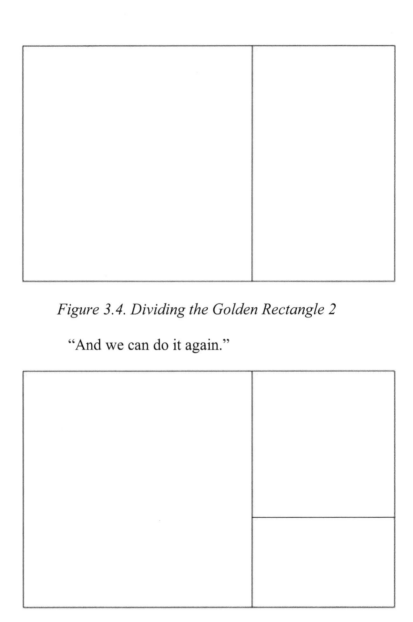

Figure 3.4. Dividing the Golden Rectangle 2

"And we can do it again."

Figure 3.5. Dividing the Golden Rectangle 3

"And again."

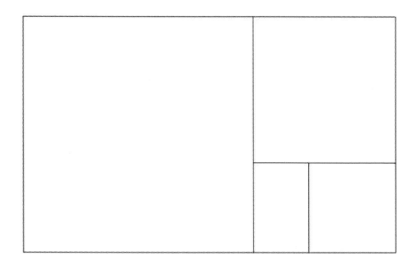

Figure 3.6. Dividing the Golden Rectangle 4

"And on and on, I'll bet," guessed Hunter.

"You're right." Grandpa replied, "And this only works with a Golden Rectangle. Let's do a bunch more:"

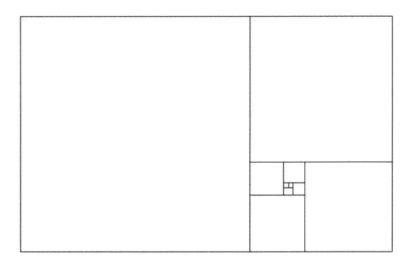

Figure 3.7. Dividing the Golden Rectangle 5

"Now, the precision of our lines and measurements isn't good enough to keep this up for long, but the smaller and smaller squares are converging to a single point. That point can be found by the intersection of any two diagonals:"

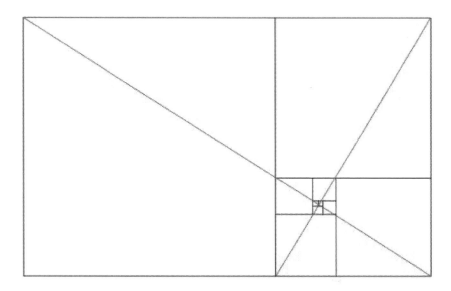

Figure 3.8. Finding the "Eye of God"

"Because of the seemingly divine nature of the Golden Ratio, a famous mathematician once recommended that we call that point the Eye of God. And when we finish exploring phi, I think you'll agree," Grandpa said.

"I'm looking forward to that," Courtney replied.

The Logarithmic Spiral

"Take a look at this – let's connect the corners of the squares together:"

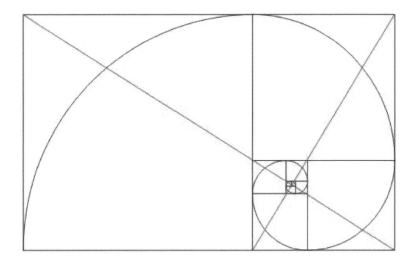

Figure 3.9. Drawing the Logarithmic Spiral

"Oh, wow!"

"Wow is right. Some people consider that curve to be one of the most beautiful shapes there are. It is a logarithmic spiral, which means that as you progress around it, its radius gets proportionally larger," Grandpa explained.

"There's that word again" said Courtney, "proportionally. And so it shouldn't be too surprising to see the connection with phi. I suppose we should call it the Golden Spiral."

"That's right," Grandpa answered, "Let's get in the car, grab a bite to eat, and stop by a shop where I want to show you something special."

"OK," Hunter agreed. "I'm starving."

"And curious," added Morgan.

"He's curious, all right," Courtney said with a smile...

After lunch, they stopped at an interior design studio Gran uses, where Grandpa had spotted some interesting accessories during his last visit.

"Over here," Grandpa called to the three of them as we were wandering around the shop admiring things. "Here's a fifty million year old fossil turned into a beautiful work of art. Look at it and tell me what you see!"

Figure 3.10. Logarithmic Fossil 1

"Oh, man," exclaimed Morgan. "That's got to be a logarithmic spiral."

"Yes," Grandpa answered, "it certainly is. And as you can imagine, it results from the proportional growth of the shell. Look over here!"

Figure 3.11. Logarithmic Fossil 2

"This one's been cut in half," said Hunter. "You can see the spiral inside."

"Yes," Grandpa said, "and since it is a fossil, meaning that minerals have turned it into stone, it shows colors and patterns when it's polished. If we cut a new, empty shell in half, we see the same structure, except it's empty."

"Is it the same with snails and other shells?" Courtney wondered.

"Yes, most shells are helical in form, and you can see many of them at the seashore or on the Internet. Do a little searching and you'll see lots of examples. Here again, we are seeing phi associated with proportional growth."

"Let's beat the traffic and head for home. I'll bet our Reader will already be on the Internet while we're driving."

"Now that we're home, I want to show you something else about the logarithmic spiral. It is also called an equiangular spiral because a line from the central point always intersects the curve at the same angle. Let's take a look."

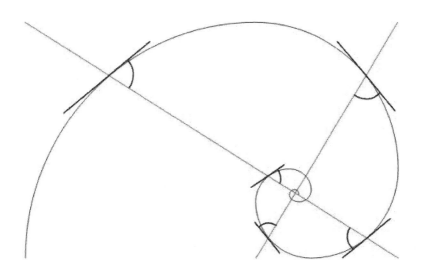

Figure 3.12. Equiangular Intersections on a
Logarithmic Spiral

"In our example here, the angle of intersection between the blue and red lines is about 50 degrees. And it's true no matter how far out the spiral progresses. The logarithmic spiral is the only curve for which this is true, which is why it is also called the equiangular spiral.

"By the way, what if the angle is 90 degrees?" asked Grandpa.

"Hey, it would make a circle!" Hunter exclaimed.

"Yes, and it wouldn't grow like the spiral – it would be a fixed diameter. So here we have a relationship that shows that a circle is a special case of a logarithmic spiral, and a connection between phi and pi, two of the most famous irrational numbers! What a surprise that is!"

Flying a 747

"Now, Hunter, you like airplanes and flying. Please bring the globe over here where we can all see it and we'll plan a flight.

"OK, let's start our flight from San Diego, and choose a destination that's not too far away. Since we are in the far southwest corner of the country, pick a city east and maybe north of here so our planning is not too complicated," Grandpa suggested.

"How about Phoenix?" Courtney offered.

"Hey, that's good," added Hunter. "While we're there we can rent a car, drive up to the Grand Canyon, and even visit some relatives in Williams."

"And Gran, Courtney and Mom can do some shopping in Scottsdale," Morgan said. "You and Dad can play golf at the resort while we swim and lie in the sun."

"Man, you guys sure can get carried away. But, OK, Phoenix is a good example here. So after we take off, what compass heading will we use to get to Phoenix?" Grandpa asked.

"I think we need a bigger map than the globe," suggested Courtney.

"I agree. Let's look at the Internet and see what we can find." Grandpa said.

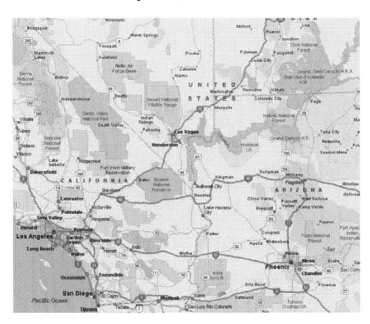

Figure 3.13. Map of Southwest

"Now let's plot our course. Hunter, can you take care of that?"

"Sure, Grandpa," he replied. "Here it is."

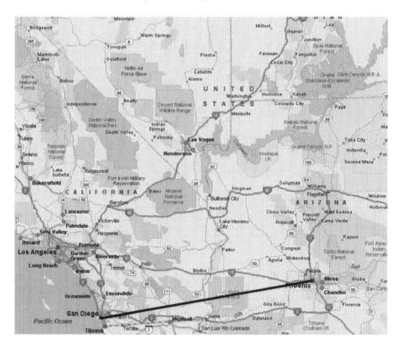

Figure 3.14. The Course to Phoenix

"OK," Grandpa replied, "Let's ignore that fact that we aren't allowed to fly over the weapons range northeast of Yuma, since we're only pretending."

"Since we're pretending," added Morgan, "why don't we fly a military plane and blow up some cactus on the way over?"

76

"Good grief," moaned Courtney.

"Now we need to know what course to dial into our GPS system so we can take off," Grandpa suggested.

"First we need to know which way is north," said Hunter.

"Right. And since our map does not have a compass rose, let's use a clue on the map. Anybody see a north-south line we can use?" Grandpa asked.

"Hmmm. Grandpa, it looks like the border between Nevada and Utah might help," offered Courtney.

"OK, let's use that, at least for our story," Grandpa agreed.

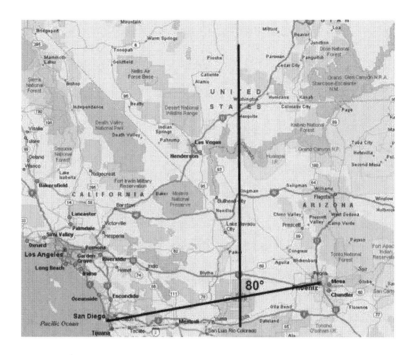

Figure 3.15. The Heading to Phoenix

"So now we see, after measuring the angle with a protractor, that our course is supposed to be 80 degrees. The way navigational headings are expressed is the angle clockwise from north," Grandpa explained. "Now ponder this question: If we fall asleep on the trip and have lots of fuel, and pass right over Phoenix without stopping, where will we wind up?"

"Well," Hunter ventured, "I guess we'd go all the way across the country, and the Atlantic Ocean, and Europe, and on and on."

"Maybe we would wind up back in San Diego," Morgan guessed.

"Yes, that seems reasonable," Courtney added. "If you go in a straight line, you would come back here."

"That's true, Courtney," Grandpa said "but will we be going in a straight line?"

"It sure looks straight to me," Morgan said.

"Yes, and the world outside looks flat, doesn't it?" Grandpa asked.

"Grandpa, that's silly," Courtney said. "Everyone knows the world is round."

"Exactly, Cort, but the straight line from San Diego to Phoenix is also deceiving. Let's plot this course on a globe."

We already had a globe, so that was the easy part, although we had to unscrew the South Pole screw to take off the mounting ring. We decided that we could use white correcting tape (Post-it) so we could mark the course without damaging the globe. Then, after some discussion, we decided to just fold a piece of paper at an 80° angle, and position it on each line of longitude. We knew the longitudinal lines ran north and south, so that provided the reference we needed. So by laying the template on each successive longitudinal line, starting at San Diego, we passed over Phoenix, and kept going.

"Hey, this is starting to curve," noticed Morgan.

"Yes, it is," Grandpa said as we passed over New York City, heading for Newfoundland.

"Oh, look!" Courtney exclaimed, "We're going over Northern Ireland and headed for Sweden."

"Better turn up the heat," Grandpa suggested, "we're about to cross the Arctic Circle."

And as we passed over the northern part of Siberia, it was clear that we weren't headed for San Diego. The spiral shape of the curve was now becoming very apparent.

"I think we are going to circle the North Pole," guessed Hunter.

"Yes, and we are going to circle it in tighter and tighter turns," Grandpa said. "And by the time we get to the pole, we are going to have the wings vertical, the turn will be so tight.

"Good thing we don't have any passengers," said Morgan, "they would be scared to death."

"Or maybe we could charge extra for the thrill," Courtney offered.

By now we were about as close to the pole of the globe as we were going to get, because the lines were getting very close together. Here's what our globe now looked like:

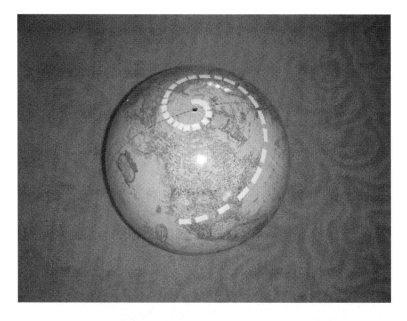

Figure 3.16. Our Flight Path

"We know that curve by now," said Morgan. "That's the same spiral."

"That's right," Grandpa said. "We created a logarithmic spiral by making use of the fact that a logarithmic spiral is an equiangular spiral, as I mentioned a while ago. And obviously, in order to fly around the world, or part of it, you have to keep changing your heading as you go. Except for two headings."

"What was that last part?" asked Courtney.

"Except for two headings. What are they?" Grandpa asked.

This didn't require too long. Maybe some of our Readers already have the answer. But after studying the globe, imagining flying in various directions in both northern and southern hemispheres, Hunter popped up with one answer.

"Ninety degrees," he announced. "You can take the long route around the equator, or go farther north or south and fly 90 degrees and take a shorter circle."

"Correct." Grandpa said. "You would be traveling on a latitudinal line. And you could also fly the other direction, west, with a heading of 270 degrees. Remember? The spiral with a 90 degree angle to its radial makes a circle!

"Speaking of degrees, I suggest we heat the oven up to 400 and fix a pizza."

"Yum," said Morgan, "then what's next?"

The Attacking Falcon

"Oh, the fun is just beginning," Grandpa replied. "Now that we've done the Golden Rectangle, we'll take a look at the Golden Triangle and see where that leads. But first I want to point out another flying machine that uses the logarithmic spiral. It's one of the fastest birds in the world; the falcon."

"When and why does he fly a logarithmic spiral?" asked Courtney. "Does he have a built-in GPS?"

"Well, maybe he does for long distance flights, Courtney, but where his spiral is well-documented is when he is attacking his prey, such as another bird in flight. He swoops down at over a hundred miles an hour in a logarithmic spiral until he snags his prey. Any ideas about what's going on?" Grandpa challenged.

"Like most birds, the falcon has an eye on each side of its head. So seeing straight ahead is not really possible. So he either has to turn his head sideways to see ahead, or he has to look slightly to the side. Now turning his head ruins his precise aerodynamics, and at his speed, it really counts. So his only option is to look at his prey slightly to the side. Forty degrees, to be exact.

"So what happens when he flies toward an object at a constant angle?" Grandpa asked.

"Oh, the constant angle!" exclaimed Hunter, "that will make him fly in a spiral, won't it?"

"Exactly right. Just like we homed in on the North Pole in our jet, he homes in on his prey in exactly the same spiral, except in a different size."

Bugs Chasing Bugs

"Here's a famous math exercise, although sometimes called with different names using bugs, mice, or beetles.

"Let's say you have four bugs at the four corners of a square, and they each head for the bug to their immediate right. Let's see what it looks like.

"Morgan, get a ruler and piece of paper for us to use. Reader, you can do the same, and follow along with us." Grandpa said.

"Draw a large square on the paper, for example, six inches on a side. Now make a dot at each corner, representing your four bugs. Now draw a line $\frac{1}{4}$ inch long from each bug headed toward the next bug. Now the next line segment will head to the left a little, because the next $\frac{1}{4}$ inch line will be headed toward the next bug's new location. Like this," Grandpa said.

So after taking turns measuring and drawing, after five segments were drawn, the bug problem looked like this:

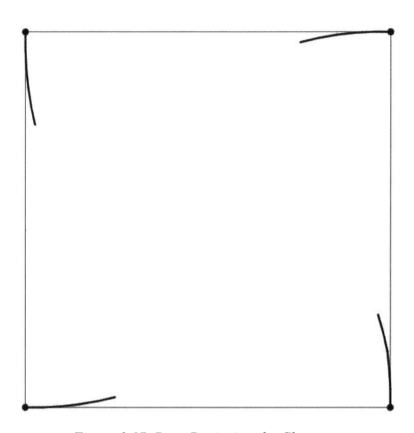

Figure 3.17. Bugs Beginning the Chase

"They're starting to curve," said Hunter. "I'll bet they will intercept each other like the falcon did."

"Yep," Courtney added, "I feel logarithmic spirals coming on."

Sure enough, we ended up with this.

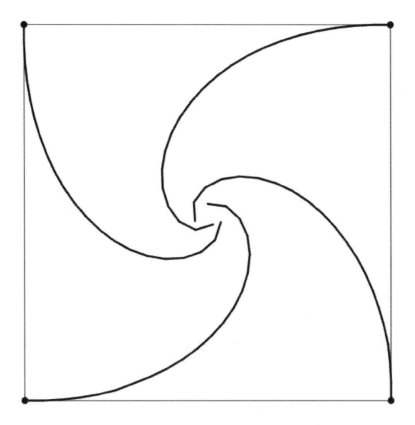

Figure 3.18. Bugs Homing in on Each Other

"It gets a little raggedy near the center, because we are using line segments, where the real bugs would be moving continuously," Grandpa said. "But the distance to their meeting point is finite, and can be calculated. By the way, you'll get these same curves if the bugs start at the corners of any regular polygon, like a triangle, square, pentagon, or hexagon.

"We're not going to work on the formula, or calculate any of the distances or times, but if you get more into mathematics, you'll find lots of references to this problem on the Internet. Here's a great reference, with animated bugs chasing each other in several different polygons: http://mathworld.wolfram.com/MiceProblem.html.

I think that's enough for now."

"I agree," commented Morgan, "and now the pizza's done. I suppose there's phi in the pizza."

"Sure," said Courtney, "haven't you ever heard of a pizza phi?"

Bernoulli's Grave

Courtney was just beginning her first course in calculus, so while they ate, Grandpa told a story about the Bernoulli brothers, generally considered the founders of the calculus. It turns out that Jakob Bernoulli, the oldest of the brothers in a Swiss family already famous for their mathematical discoveries, did a lot of work involving the logarithmic spiral, and considered it so fundamentally beautiful that he wished it engraved on his grave marker.

Figure 3.19. Bernoulli's Grave Marker

When he died in 1705, the stone engraver, without realizing what he was doing, mistakenly engraved the arithmetic spiral we see above.

"Should have planned ahead." noted Morgan. "He obviously needed an engraver who knew more about mathematics."

"By the way," Grandpa said, "the words engraved around the spiral are *eadem mutata resurgo* which mean 'I shall arise the same though changed'. 'Same' and 'changed' in the same sentence. I think he's left us with a puzzle…"

Chapter 4. Drawing Stars

Before starting the Golden Triangle fun, Grandpa thought it would be a good idea to review the principle of geometric construction. They had used construction methods to generate the Golden Rectangle in the last chapter, but the principle is far more general and useful than that.

"What does geometric construction really mean, Grandpa?" asked Courtney. "I know construction means building – but you mean something more specific here, I'm sure."

"That's right", Grandpa replied. "Geometric construction refers to drawing geometric figures using only a straight edge and a compass. A ruler can be used as a straight edge, but the rulings on it (the numbers and other marks) must be ignored. One reason is that no matter how precise and expensive the ruler is, you won't be able to find 1.333333…. on it, much less pi (π) or phi (φ). But the main reason is that in order to use construction as part of a mathematical or geometrical proof, you don't want arguments over how a scale is read or who made it or to what precision. Let's look at a few examples, some of which you will be able to use in real life.

"Bisecting a line, which we did in the last chapter to create the Golden Rectangle, is easy even when you don't have a tape measure or ruler, as long as you have the necessary straight edge and compass. And I don't mean a compass that tells us which way is north, by the way, I mean a drawing instrument! Morgan, please see if you can find my old compass in that drawer, and I'll get a ruler we can use as a straight edge.

Constructing the Golden Rectangle and Golden Triangle

"Let's start by drawing a straight line. Reader, why don't you join us?"

Hunter drew the straight line on a piece of paper, and Morgan was successful at finding a compass.

Figure 4.1. Bisecting a Line Step 1

"OK, now we have the line. Now, Hunter, put the point of the compass at one end of the line and extend the marking end a little past where you think the middle of the line would be. Now draw a little arc above and below the line, long enough so that the arc will be above and below where you think the center point is going to be."

"Like this, Grandpa?" he asked.

Figure 4.2. Bisecting a Line Step 2

"Perfect", Grandpa replied. "Now do the same from the other end of the line, so that the arcs intersect."

Figure 4.3. Bisecting a Line Step 3

"Now the last step is to connect the two points where the arcs intersect, and you have the mid-point of the line where the two lines cross."

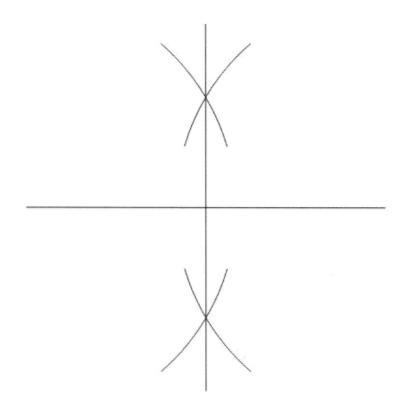

Figure 4.4. Bisecting a Line Step 4

"Gee, that was easy," commented Courtney.

"Yes," Grandpa replied, "and there's an extra bonus here. You have also used geometric construction to draw a right angle, since the new line is at 90° to the first line. Now if you wanted to build something big, like a building or a pyramid before there was fancy surveying equipment, ropes pulled straight for a straight

95

edge and ropes pulled tight around an anchor to make a compass would help you make the building square."

"So we would use geometric construction for pyramid or temple construction," offered Morgan.

"You bet. And houses and boats. We'll see more examples as we go along. But now it's time to investigate the Golden Triangle."

"Do we make it by construction?" asked Courtney.

"Aha, you remembered that we made the Golden Rectangle by construction, didn't you? Let's take a look at that again." Grandpa said.

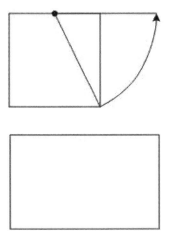

Figure 4.5. Construction of the Golden Rectangle

"This is how we derived the Golden Rectangle from a simple square. We bisected the top edge, and used a compass to create the new length of the top side. Now turn the Golden Rectangle on its end so our Golden Triangle will be vertical."

"Now let's use our compass to tip the sides in toward the center:"

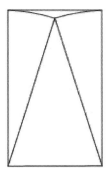

"And where they meet is the apex of the Golden Triangle. So we wind up with a triangle that looks like this:"

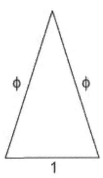

Figure 4.6. The Golden Triangle

"And the sides are one, phi, and phi, which is where the Golden part comes in, I suppose," guessed Morgan.

"Yes", Grandpa replied, "and remember that when we say 1 and phi, we are talking about the ratio, or proportion of the lengths. For example, if the base of the triangle was 10 inches long, what would each side be?"

"16.18 inches," Hunter replied.

"Right on," Grandpa replied. "You must be taking notes. There's also something interesting about the angles we should notice. As you know, the angles of any triangle must add up to 180°. Did you know that?"

"I did," replied Hunter and Courtney.

"I do now," added Morgan.

"And you probably also realize that this is an isosceles triangle, which means what?" Grandpa tested.

"Two equal sides," replied Courtney.

"Right," I said, "iso is a prefix that means equal. On weather maps, isobars are lines of equal pressure, for example. Isosceles triangles also have two equal interior angles opposite the equal sides. For our Golden Triangle, the two bottom angles are each 72° and the apex angle is 36°. Notice anything interesting about those numbers?"

"Let's see," said Morgan, reaching for the calculator. "Sure enough, they add up to 180°, like they should."

"Hey," Hunter exclaimed, "72 is twice 36!"

"Funny, huh?" Grandpa asked. "And it's the only triangle like that. Now look what happens if we bisect one of the larger angles:"

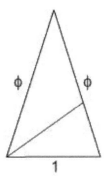

Figure 4.7. The Golden Gnomon

"In the lower left corner we have bisected the 72° angle, which leaves us with two 36° angles. And lying on its side is another isosceles triangle with a 36° degree apex angle. Do you know what that means?"

"Holy smoke!" exclaimed Courtney. "That must be another Golden Triangle, then. If its apex is also 36°, then the other two must be 72°."

"Yes," Grandpa said, "if the other side is 1, which it is."

"Prove it," requested Morgan.

"Later," Grandpa replied with a smile and a wink. "Now notice the other new triangle, which is also an isosceles. It has φ as its base, and two sides equal to

1. It has an apex angle of 108°, because, as you can see, the corner of the new Golden Triangle (which is 72°, and the other angles all lie on a straight line, so they must total 180°. And $180 - 72 = 108$. This new triangle, with sides ϕ, 1, and 1, is often called the Golden Gnomon. That's pronounced "No Mon". Sounds kinda Scottish, doesn't it?"

"Yes, Mon," answered Hunter.

"Is that a triangle? No, Mon, that's a gnomon," added Courtney.

After we recovered from that, the inevitable happened. "What's a gnomon?" asked Morgan.

"Go ask your mother," Grandpa answered. "Just kidding. I knew one of you would ask that, so I looked it up. There are two meanings. One is the arm on a sundial that casts a shadow on the sundial face. The other meaning is the part of a figure that is left after a similar piece is cut off. So it kind of means "leftover".

"Do you remember how we could whack a square off of a Golden Rectangle and wind up with another Golden Rectangle? Well, we have a similar situation here. Let's draw a larger Golden Triangle, give Hunter a ruler, and let him go nuts."

"He's nuts anyhow", commented Courtney.

"Watch this, doubters," replied Hunter.

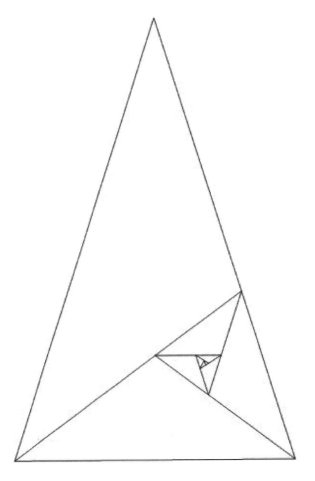

Figure 4.8. Golden Triangle Sections

"Now there's an absolutely beautiful work of art," Grandpa said. "Also notice the vanishing point, similar to the God's Eye in the Golden Rectangle."

"Hey, I'll bet we can draw another spiral," guessed Morgan.

"OK, let's do it." Grandpa replied. "Let's connect the corners of the gnomons."

"Drum roll, please," requested Courtney. "Ta-da!"

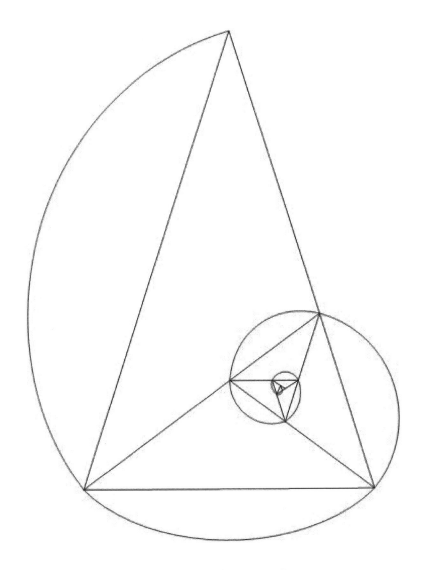

Figure 4.9. Another Spiral!

Pentagons and Pentagraphs

"But wait," Grandpa said. "Before you call and order this, look at what else the Golden Triangle can do! Let's put five of them together with their corners touching. Now this gives us a pentagon surrounded by Golden Triangles:"

Figure 4.10. A Pentagraph (Star)

"Wow. Are you saying that a star and a pentagon use the Golden Ratio ϕ?" asked Courtney.

"Yep," Grandpa replied, "not just use them, but they are defined by them. By the way, the geometric name of the star is pentagram, also sometimes called a pentacle, and the relationship between the pentagram, the pentagon, and phi has been known and marveled at for centuries.

"We are really up to our ears in ϕ in this figure. For example, not only is each point on the star a Golden Triangle, but you'll see three Golden Gnomons in there as well. Here, let's mark one of them:"

Figure 4.11. A Golden Gnomon in a Pentagraph

"Now, Morgan, please use the straight edge and connect the five points of the pentagram. Let's see what we get."

So he did, and here is the result:

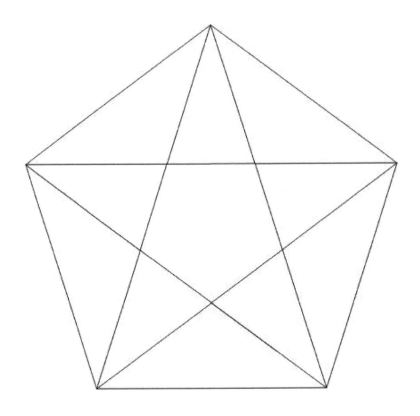

Figure 4.12. Another Pentagon!

"Whoa, another pentagon," exclaimed Hunter.

"And," Grandpa added, "ten more Golden Triangles:"

"And, let's see... ten more Golden Gnomons," said Courtney.

"I only see five gnomons," said Morgan.

"Let's take a closer look," Grandpa suggested, "there are five small ones tucked in between each point of the star, and there are five larger ones that connect every other point of the star. Here, let's mark one sample of each with colors, red for the Golden Triangles and blue for the Golden Gnomons."

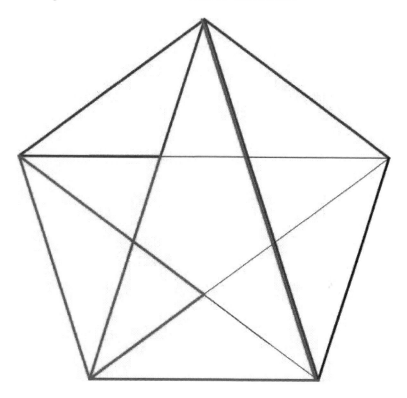

Figure 4.13. Finding Golden Triangles and Golden Gnomons

"OK, Morgan, here's another job for you. Use the straight edge again and connect every other apex of the interior pentagon for us," Grandpa asked.

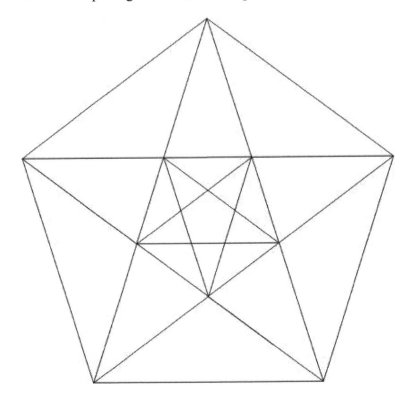

Figure 4.14. More Stars and Pentagons

"Another pentagram! And another pentagon! I think this could go on and on. Right, Grandpa?" asked Hunter.

"You're absolutely right, Hunter. Just like the other figures we've explored, we can keep generating the pattern over and over, both larger and smaller. And if you would like to have a contest, make three copies of this figure, and each of you count the numbers of Golden Triangles and Golden Gnomons you can find. Let's challenge the Reader to do the same. I believe there are 40 Golden Triangles and 45 Golden Gnomons. See if you can find them all!" Grandpa challenged.

"Next time we get together, we are going to explore the interior angles and learn more about the pentagon. In the meantime, I suggest you get some colored pencils to keep track of the triangles you count!"

Folding Paper

"Oh, by the way," said Grandpa, "there's another surprising way to create a pentagon."

Grandpa cut a long strip along one side of a piece of printer paper, about ½ inch wide.

"Now, Courtney, carefully tie a simple overhand knot in the paper strip. Be careful not to tear the paper, and as it gets tight, crease the paper so that the knot lies flat."

And here's what she got.

Figure 4.15. A Paper Knot

Figure 4.16. A Paper Pentagon (with its lower left edge hidden)

"Now we have a little pentagon knot with a Golden Triangle in the upper left part. In fact, if you hold it up to the light, you can see several Golden Triangles and Golden Gnomons," suggested Grandpa.

Surprised? There's even phi in a knot!

113

Chapter 5. Phi in the Garden

A couple of weeks later, Grandpa and the kids were all together again for an afternoon of barbeque and swimming. They were pulling some weeds here and there in the garden while Morgan was busy finding Fibonacci numbers in flowers and leaf patterns. We also picked some tomatoes and squash to add to our dinner menu.

"Grandpa," Courtney said, "we constantly see spirals, Fibonacci numbers and even pentagons in natural growing things. What's going on?"

"Well," Grandpa replied, "pretty soon we'll see that it has to do with efficiency, I believe. Nature is designed to reward efficiency. "

Grandpa pointed to a bee crawling around the blossoms of the lima bean vine.

"I think not just in plants, but also in animals. Would you be surprised to find Fibonacci and phi hiding in a bee colony?

"Let's get finished here and go back inside."

Hunter had a frown on his face.

"Grandpa," he said, "I've been looking at bee hives on the Internet and the honeycombs aren't pentagons, liked I hoped. They're hexagons – every cell has six sides. Six isn't a Fibonacci number."

"That's right. And of course there's a reason for that," Grandpa replied.

"We need to change subjects for a little while and talk about tiling."

Tiling

"Tiling?" Morgan asked. "Like floor tile?"

"Yep," Grandpa replied, "tiling, as a mathematical term, refers to arranging geometrical shapes on a flat plane, like the floor."

"Or like cells in a honeycomb," offered Courtney

"Right. But there are only a few shapes that you can use without leaving gaps or odd spaces, and that look the same from all direction. This is called *periodic* tiling. Want to guess at some shapes that work?" Grandpa asked.

116

"The floor is made of rectangles, like a brick wall pattern," said Hunter.

"Yes, and that's a four-sided figure, but it looks different depending on which way is up. But if the rectangles are squares, it works. So if we want to list shapes that permit periodic tiling, let's count the square as one.

"Here's a pad of graph paper. Who wants to volunteer to make a diagram of tiling with squares?" asked Grandpa.

Courtney volunteered, explaining that when she grew up she wanted to be an interior designer like Gran.

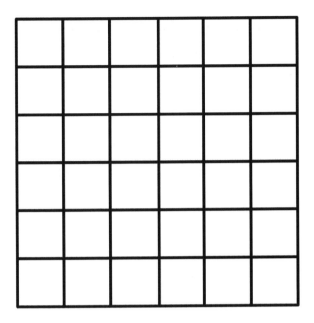

Figure 5.1. Tiling with Squares

"I think you can tile with triangles," said Courtney.

"Yes," said Hunter, "just draw some diagonal lines through the squares."

So she did, this is what the result looked like.

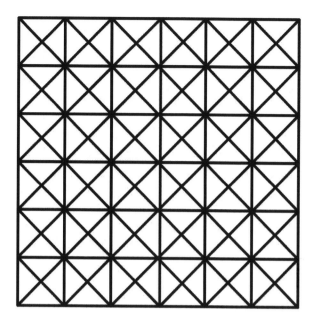

Figure 5.2. Making Triangular Tiles

"Now when you look at this figure, what do you see?" Grandpa asked.

"Lots of triangles and squares of lots of sizes!" replied Morgan.

"Yes, and squares tilted at 45 degrees, too," said Hunter.

So Grandpa invited the kids, along with the Reader, to mark some of these.

After only a few minutes, they had some samples of hidden tiled triangles and squares.

119

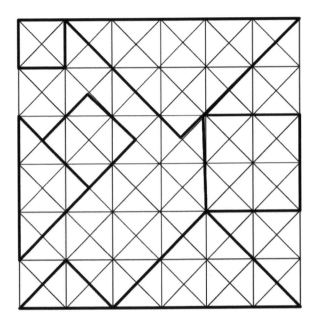

Figure 5.3. Finding squares and triangles

"There's another specific triangle that is important for tiling, and that's an equilateral triangle. What does "equilateral" mean?" asked Grandpa.

"All three sides equal," replied Hunter. "Let's make some tiles."

"I want to draw these," said future draftsman/engineer Morgan.

"OK, let's get to work. And let's invite our Reader to do the same," Grandpa said.

So Hunter drew a line horizontally one inch long, following the grid marked on the graph paper. But it was hard to get the other two sides the same, and at the same time equal to the length of the base of the triangle.

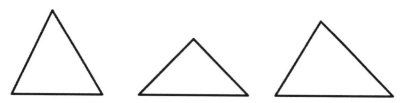

Figure 5.4. Triangle Trouble

"I can't just follow the lines on graph paper. So I need some other way," moaned Morgan.

"Maybe from the ends of the base we could draw a certain angle," suggested Hunter. "And then just draw them up until they meet. But what's the angle?"

"OK, Courtney," Grandpa said, "what's the angle? All three sides are equal, so what does that tell you about the angles."

"Oh, I know! They also have to also be equal," Courtney replied.

"So what is the angle?" Grandpa asked again.

Hunter said, "They have to add up to 180 degrees, like any triangle, so they must each be 60 degrees!"

"Right. But if we don't have a draftsman's triangle, or a computer drawing software program, or a protractor, what can we do? Can we do it by construction, like we (and the ancients) made figures using only a straight edge and a compass?" asked Grandpa.

Constructing an Equilateral Triangle

"Here's how we solve that problem," said Grandpa. "Let's think about it for a minute. If we have the baseline, which is easy, what do we know about the missing two sides? Well, first of all, where do they meet?"

"In the middle, right over the center of the base," offered Morgan.

"Hey," said Hunter, "we learned how to find the center of a line already."

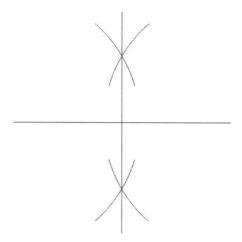

Figure 5.5. Bisecting the Base

Reader, if you can't remember how we did it, you can review the method back when we were constructing the Golden Rectangle.

"Now," Grandpa said, "what else do we know about the equilateral triangle, in addition to the fact that they will intersect on that vertical line we just drew?"

"Oh!" Courtney exclaimed, "Each side will be equal to the base, so we can use the compass again."

"Show us," Grandpa asked.

So Courtney drew another arc with the compass, using the base of the triangle as the radius:

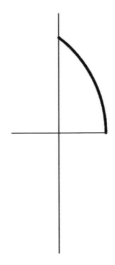

Figure 5.6. Swinging the Arc

"Now we know where the other two sides meet," said Hunter, "I'll finish the triangle."

Figure 5.7. Finishing the Triangle

"Wow – there it is!" said Morgan. "Now to tile the floor we just need 1,000 more!"

"Yep," said Grandpa, "we sure can't do this for every one! That's why we do pattern making. Let's cut it out of the paper and use it as a pattern."

So they did. And they took turns drawing triangles using their cut-out pattern as the template, with a few breaks for snacks, and eventually came up with a tiling pattern consisting of equilateral triangles.

Tiling a Beehive

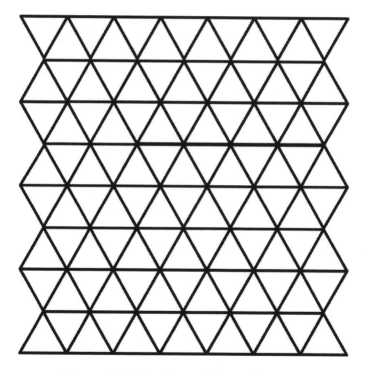

Figure 5.8. Equilateral Triangle Tiling

"Remember how we saw hidden patterns in the square tiling?" Grandpa asked.

"Yep, we saw triangles, and squares of all sizes," replied Morgan.

"And what do we see here, in addition to lots of sizes of triangles?"

"I see honeycomb cells!" exclaimed Hunter.

"And they seem to tile perfectly," said Courtney, "look!"

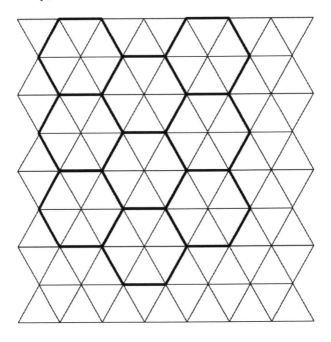

Figure 5.9. Honeycomb Tiling

"That looks just like a photo I just saw of a real honeycomb," said Hunter.

Figure 5.10. A Real Honeycomb

"Perfect tiling of perfect hexagons," marveled Grandpa." Where do you suppose the bees got the straightedges, compasses, paper, and scissors to make their template?"

Man, that shut everyone up for a few minutes.

"Holy smoke!" Courtney exclaimed, "can you imagine how tiny their little brains are? And that's only the construction of their home."

"And they know how to live together, to fly miles to find flowers, and to find their way home, and to tell each other where the flowers are," added Grandpa. "And in their spare time, they have babies and make honey. And they make babies according to the Fibonacci series!"

"You mean there's phi in the way bees multiply?" asked Morgan.

"Yep. Let's look into that later," replied Grandpa.

We decided to take a dinner break while pondering these miraculous things.

"Grandpa," said Morgan, "where's phi in the beehive hexagons?"

"OK, here's the thing. Let's consider tiling first, and then the bees." Grandpa said.

"So far we've constructed periodic tilings using tiles with three and four sides. But you see in the last example, we can also tile with six-sided tiles, or hexagons. So do the bees!

"Now if you think about it, you realize that the more sides a figure has, the more inside area it has. Like a balloon, as the sides push out, the area inside increases."

"Until it becomes a circle!" exclaimed Courtney.

"Right. But you can't tile circles efficiently, because they don't nest together. Even putting them together into a hexagonal pattern, like a stack of oranges in the market, the wasted space between them still wastes about 20% of the available area.

"Now if you have your choice between only three, four, or six sides, you'll choose six. Which the bees do, probably because it's the most efficient shape," said Grandpa. "I think we're going to discover that phi is in nature for that very reason – efficiency."

"Grandpa," asked Morgan, "what happened to our favorite – the pentagon?"

"Yep, the pentagon is missing. You can't make a periodic tiling of pentagons no matter how hard you try. But does that mean that tilings cannot contain phi?"

After thinking about this, Hunter said, "Well, if we can tile with triangles, why can't we tile with Golden Triangles?"

"Or Golden Rectangles," added Courtney.

"Yes, to both. And if we disregard the periodic requirement, a famous mathematician named Roger Penrose found a way to tile with golden gnomons, in the shapes of what he named "kites" and "darts".

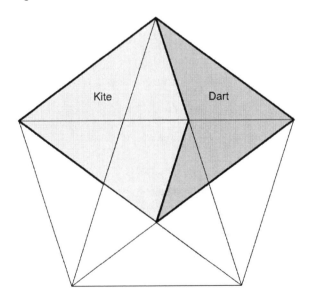

Figure 5.11. Penrose Kite and Dart

130

"There are complicated mathematical papers on this subject, and I recommend that you and the Reader Google 'Penrose Kites and Darts' if you want to explore more. Some of it is pretty advanced, though.

"But we're kind of forcing phi into these tilings, and they don't happen in nature, as far as I can tell. We need to distinguish between growing things and constructed things. We tile a floor or wall, and bees tile a honeycomb. Neither of these things is growing. They are being built. See the difference?" asked Grandpa.

"Want to see a tiled pentagon? Look here," as Grandpa led the kids into the kitchen.

Figure 5.12. Pineapple Tiles

"Of course, they are not perfect, and are kind of mushed together. But they have five sides, and lend themselves to creating the spirals we noticed earlier.

"So phi and its associated figures pentagons and spirals are connected to growing things. Do you think there are growing things outside of nature?" asked Grandpa.

"Outside of nature?" said Hunter, with a grin, "do you mean supernatural?"

Grandpa laughed. "Yes, Hunter, supernatural is outside of nature, but that's not quite what I mean. I mean real-world, but not natural growing things. I think we need to learn about fractals."

Fractals

"That word sounds related to fractions," commented Courtney.

"Yes, you're right. Let's 'grow' something on paper," said Grandpa.

"Fractals are created by starting with a figure, and adding to it a smaller version of the same shape. For example, let's start with a line one inch long, and add two lines each ½ inch long at 120 degrees to each other so they are spaced evenly.

"Morgan, start a fresh sheet of graph paper and let's do this, along with our Reader."

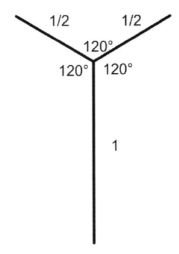

Figure 5.13. Fractal Tree Stage One

"Now let's do it again

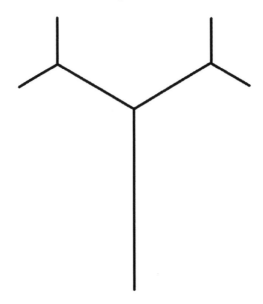

Figure 5.14. Fractal Tree Stage Two

"Now two more times."

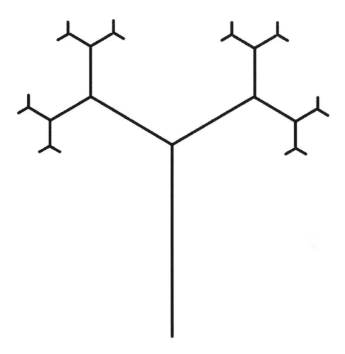

Figure 5.15. Fractal Tree Stage Three

"OK, we're going to get worn out continuing this. But it's not too hard to program a computer to do this, and lots of people have done it. Let's take a look at some of them from the Internet," suggested Grandpa. "Many people have programmed computers to make fractal images, and they are amazingly like natural plants."

Everyone got on the 'net, and found lots of examples of fractals.

"They look like plants!" said Morgan.

"I think we were about to make a tree, if we kept going," added Hunter.

Sure enough, many of the fractals looked like trees, broccoli, ferns, and many other plants.

Figure 5.16. Fractal Tree

Figure 5.17. Fractal Fern

"Many images like these are available from places like www.mathartfun.com, and I recommend you and the Reader spend some time checking out this interesting connection between math and nature," said Grandpa.

"Where's phi?" asked Courtney.

"Can you stand another surprise?" asked Grandpa.

"Sure, Grandpa," replied Hunter, "Bring it on!"

"OK," Grandpa replied, "look at the tree in the picture two figures back. See how the branches in the middle overlap each other? Now remember that when we started we used ½ the length of each branch to create the next two. If we measure the ratio for that picture, we find that they used 0.666, instead of 0.5. What happens to the tree if we make that ratio larger or smaller?"

"I think the smaller number will make the tree have many little branches on each stem, so the tree will be kind of spindly," suggested Morgan.

"Exactly," replied Grandpa, "and larger numbers will make it denser with more overlapping branches. Now it turns out that you can calculate the exact ratio that will make the branches eventually touch each other without overlapping."

"Uh oh," said Morgan, "I can feel it coming."

"You've got it, Morgan," said Grandpa, "the number is 0.618..., which is exactly $1/\phi$! You can see the fairly simple proof of this in Mario Livio's excellent book *The Golden Ratio*. I recommend you and the Reader get a copy to learn more amazing facts about phi."

"OK, now based on what we've learned so far, why would phi be involved in this branching fractal?" asked Grandpa.

"It must have something to do with efficiency," guessed Hunter.

"Sure," replied Courtney, "for leaves, it gives the most number without crowding, maybe."

"Yes, and we'll even see phi in the angles that leaves are arranged around a stem, to allow the most light to get to each leaf. And this is in real nature, not man-made fractal nature. We can study fractals some other time, and see how they are related to more than just leaves and stems, but also tree lines and coastlines.

"So fractals are growing things made by drawing, either by hand or, preferably, with a computer.

139

OK, so much for non-nature growing things. Let's get back to nature," said Grandpa.

Back to the Bees

"We've seen that the bees' honeycombs use hexagons, and since the honeycomb is constructed, rather than grown, it doesn't involve phi. But what IS growing inside the hive?" asked Grandpa.

"Well, the bees are growing," suggested Hunter, "at least until they are grown up."

"What else is growing in size?" asked Grandpa.

"Oh," said Courtney, "the hive is growing! There are more bees all the time, aren't there?"

"Yes," said Grandpa, "that's it. The bees are multiplying. Do you remember the rabbits multiplying, and how it involved Fibonacci numbers, and, of course, phi?"

"Yes," Hunter replied, "but they don't really multiply that way."

"That's true," replied Grandpa, "That was a math problem invented by Fibonacci himself. I wonder if he would be surprised by the way bees multiply?"

"But the bees don't multiply in pairs, like rabbits," said Courtney, "there's only one queen, isn't there?"

"That's right, Courtney," replied Grandpa, "let's look at how it really works.

"There are only two rules: First, a male bee has only one parent, which is a female. Second, a female bee has two parents, a male and a female."

"Are you making this up?" said Hunter, with a smile.

"No, this is really the way it works," replied Grandpa, "Ask any bee.

"Let's make a chart, and to make it as simple as possible, we'll draw a family tree, only upside down so we can start with a single bee. Then we'll progress down the chart to his parents, grandparents, and so forth."

So they got a piece of paper and started the chart.

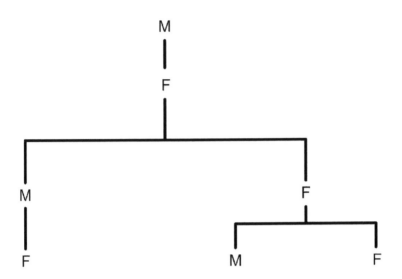

Figure 5.18. Four Generations of Bees

They drew the chart so that each male had only a female parent, and each female bee had two, one male and one female.

Eventually, they had a pretty big chart:

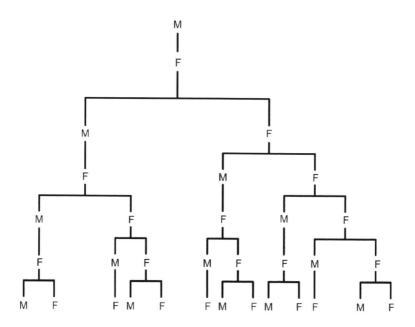

Figure 5.19. Bee Family Tree

"OK," Grandpa said, "let's count the bees. Make a list of the number of males in each generation and the number of females. Also, write down the total number of bees in each generation."

So in practically no time, they had the list:

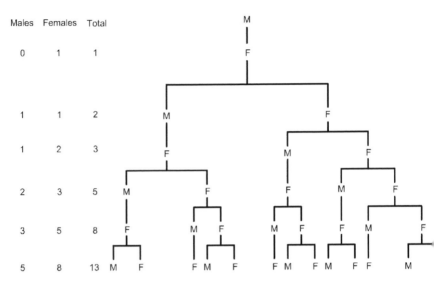

Figure 5.20. Bee Family Fibonacci Numbers

By now, everyone (probably including the Reader!) will recognize the numbers on the left. Sure enough, the number of males, the number of females, and the total number of bees in the genealogical tree are all Fibonacci numbers, in the correct order!

Branching Plants

"Now here's another surprise," said Grandpa, "If you turn that diagram over, it looks like a plant branching, doesn't it?"

Everyone agreed that, yes, the bee family tree looks like a plant without leaves!

144

"Would you believe that plants really do that?" asked Grandpa.

"By now, I'm ready to believe almost anything," remarked Morgan.

"What happens with many plants is that when a stem is ready to sprout again, it takes a rest while an adjacent one sprouts, and then it divides. So this 'taking turns' winds up looking just like the pattern we see above, only inverted. One of the most popular examples of this is a plant called the sneezewort. And, yes, it has that name because it makes people sneeze. The plant grows wild in many parts of the world, and is native to England. It is also an ingredient in one of the potions in Harry Potter! This is what it looks like:

Figure 5.21. Sneezewort

"If you study this drawing a little, you'll see the pattern. Laid out diagrammatically, it looks like this:

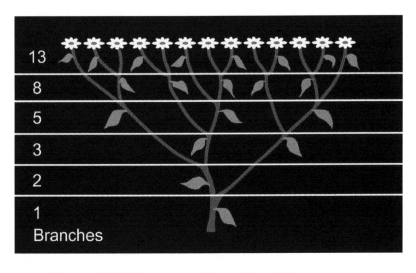

Figure 5.22. Sneezewort Branching Diagram

"I'm sure you won't have any trouble recognizing the Fibonacci numbers on the left side of the diagram," said Grandpa. "This is a very popular diagram for people who study this kind of thing, and by Googling 'sneezewort' and selecting 'pictures' you'll see lots of examples.

"While you are on the Internet, go to Jill Britton's site (http://britton.disted.camosun.bc.ca/ fibslide/jbfibslide.htm). Here you'll see examples of flower petals like we found in the garden, but she has examples of every Fibonacci number of petals, from one to 34! She teaches math at a college in Victoria, B.C., Canada, and has lots of fun math demonstrations and projects.

"Now let's take a look at some three-dimensional solids, some art, and some architecture, watching for phi!"

Chapter 6. Things Big and Small

"Way back before cell phones or even television, there was a guy named Plato, who lived in Greece in 400 B.C., about 2,600 years ago," Grandpa said.

"Grandpa, we know enough about history to know about Plato," said Courtney, with a grin.

"OK, Pythagoras, who was one of the fathers of geometry, already appreciated the Golden Ratio, the pentagon, and the pentagram. So much so that his followers used the pentagram star as the symbol of his fellowship. The pentagram represented Health. And the Golden Rectangle was considered the most appealing shape, and was used in many designs, as we'll see later.

"They recognized five solid figures, made up of squares, triangles, and pentagons. There are only five of these, and they are called the Platonic Solids. The first of these five solids is the tetrahedron.

The Tetrahedron

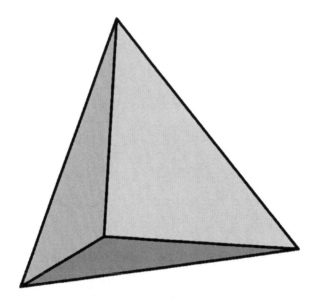

Figure 6.1. The Tetrahedron

"It is a pyramid made of equilateral triangles, so that every edge is of equal length," continued Grandpa.

"How many faces and vertices does it have," he asked.

After a few seconds, Hunter replied "I count four of each."

"And edges?" asked Grandpa.

"Six," replied Morgan.

"OK," Grandpa said, "just to learn a little thing about the Platonic Solids, let's make a note of those numbers. And where does the tetrahedron's name come from?"

"Tetra is the prefix for 'four', I think," Courtney guessed, "and there are four faces and vertices."

"That's correct, Courtney," said Grandpa, "and as we'll see, it's the faces that count.

"The next Platonic Solid is the hexahedron."

The Hexahedron

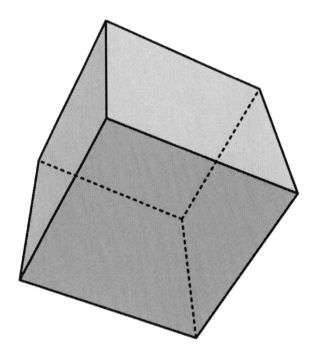

Figure 6.2. The Hexahedron

"That's a cube," said Courtney.

"Correct," replied Grandpa, "And the faces, vertices, and edges?"

"Six faces," said Morgan.

"And eight vertices," said Courtney.

"And ten edges," added Hunter.

"And its name comes from?" asked Grandpa.

"Oh, hex means six, like in hexagon, so it must just be the sides that are used in its name," said Morgan.

"Right," Grandpa said, "and the third Platonic Solid is the octahedron:"

The Octahedron

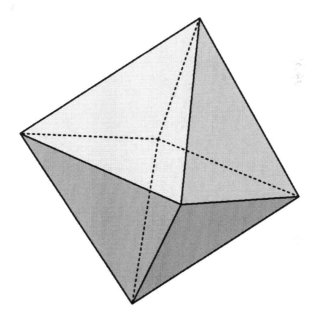

Figure 6.3. The Octahedron

"It looks like two tetrahedrons glued together," remarked Hunter.

153

"I've got the specs," said Courtney, "it's got six vertices, eight faces, and 12 edges."

"So the 'octa' prefix comes from the number of faces, sure enough," said Morgan.

"Yep," Grandpa replied, "and the fourth Platonic Solid is the icosahedron:"

The Icosahedron

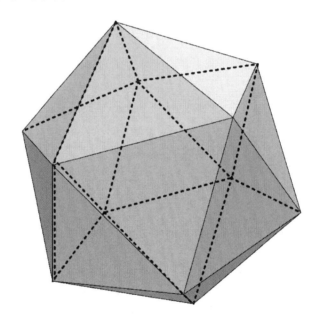

Figure 6.4. The Icosahedron

"I'm going to light the barbeque while you guys (and the Reader) count the features of the icosahedron. Also, this solid's name does not refer to the number of

154

sides, like the others. Any clues about the name?" asked Grandpa.

Grandpa came back into the house after the fire was started, and saw that a lot of drawing and marking and counting had been going on.

"OK," said Hunter, "as chairman of the icosahedron committee, I would like to report that there are 12 vertices, 20 faces, and 30 edges. And it is made of isosceles triangles, which is how it got its name."

"Good work," said Grandpa, "and there's only one more Platonic Solid. It's my favorite, the dodecahedron!"

The Dodecahedron

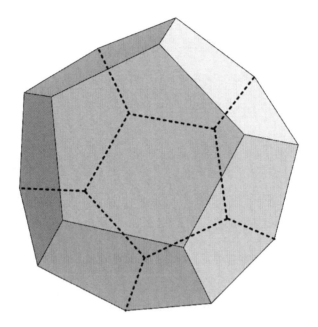

Figure 6.5. The Dodecahedron

"Yay," cheered Courtney, "it's made of pentagons!"

"Yes," Grandpa said, "and it's the last of the Platonic solids. And more amazing, there are no more possible regular geometric solids. That's it, no mas: we have three made out of triangles, one made out of squares, and one made out of pentagons.

"To save some time, I'll tell you that the dodecahedron has 20 vertices, 12 faces, and 30 edges. And, yes, 'dodeca' is 12," said Grandpa.

"'Dec' for ten and 'do' for two," added Morgan.

"Now consider the interesting fact that on paper you can draw an infinite number of multi-sided polygons with any number of sides, from three (triangle), four (square), five (pentagon, six (hexagon), and on and on until you approach a sphere. But there are five and only five *regular* polyhedra in three-dimensional space.

"We can't go into all of it now, but they nest inside each other, sometimes one forms the other when the centers of the faces are joined by a line, and so forth. Google a few of the key words here and you'll see what I mean."

"I can see that the dodecahedron involves phi," said Courtney, "because of the pentagons. But what about the others?"

"We don't want to get into too much detailed math here, but phi is involved in the areas and volumes of four of the five.

157

"Historically, these five figures have been known for ages, and in spite of them being named after Plato, complete model sets of the five solids have been discovered in prehistoric England, at some of the stone rings sites, similar to Stonehenge. If they really go back that far, their history is more like 4,000 years instead of a mere 2,600.

"Plato believed that these structures represented the elements of the universe. Because they were so limited in number, and the fact that they can be nested within each other and spheres, they were believed to be the fundamental symbols representing the basic elements of the universe at the time, namely earth, fire, water, and air. But there are five solids! There is obviously a missing element.

"Specifically, the pointy tetrahedron represented fire, the stable-looking cube, (the hexahedron) represented earth, and the octahedron, water. That left the greatest of the five to represent the universe, or ether (aether) or something.

"In the early 1600's Johannes Kepler made a model of the solar system using the Platonic solids.

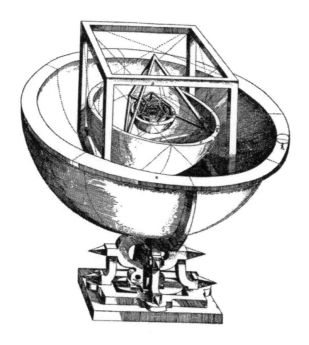

Figure 6.6. Kepler's Solar System

"But as the orbits of the planets continued to prove him wrong, he continued to insist he was right. We not only know now how wrong it was, but it was even considered crazy at the time. Galileo once remarked that he was such a nut that he should be "hissed of the stage" when he presented his theories

"His mother, Katherina, was a strange woman, and was even put on trial for the capital offense of witchcraft. Johannes helped his mother get acquitted, and both were considered what we today would call

159

weirdos. But even so, Kepler is considered to be the father of modern science."

"How could a guy so wrong on the construction of the solar system wind up the father of modern science? asked Hunter.

Grandpa explained, "He eventually became convinced that his model was wrong, and Copernicus was right. He studied the orbits, and wrote a 100-page analysis of the orbit of Mars in what he called 'my war with Mars'. (He had a sense of humor; remember that Mars is the God of War!) He understood how fundamental phi is, and studied its importance in geometry and nature. He was the one who discovered that any consecutive Fibonacci numbers converge on the Golden Ratio as the numbers get larger. But the most important thing historically was that he proved that the planet's orbits are not circles, but ellipses, with the sun at one of the foci.

"It took none other than the great Sir Isaac Newton to prove that the planetary orbits are the way they are because of the effects of gravity.

"Anyhow, I want to mention one more thing about Plato. He figured that if the Platonic Solids were as fundamental as they are, and represented air, fire, water, and earth, that you should be able to do "chemistry" with them. Because if you heat water with fire, you get air. At least that's the way it seemed. So by calculating the numbers of faces of each of the figures, he decided that water (icosahedron) equals two air (octahedron) plus fire (tetrahedron). In numbers of faces, sure enough, $20 = 2x8 + 4$. Of course, now we know that water equals two hydrogen atoms and one oxygen atom (H_2O)."

"So evidently, the octahedron should be hydrogen, not air, and the tetrahedron should be oxygen, not fire," noted Courtney, with a smirk.

We got kind of a geeky kick out of that, since hydrogen is a gas, and oxygen is necessary for combustion.

The Last Supper

"Plato assigned the dodecahedron to the universe as a whole, and in his words the dodecahedron is that 'which the god used for the embroidering the

161

constellations on the whole heaven'. For this reason, the great artist Salvador Dali, in 1955, painted the 'The Sacrament of the Last Supper' taking place within a huge dodecahedron," said Grandpa.

Figure 6.7. Salvador Dali's "The Sacrament of the Last Supper"

"This world-famous painting is 267 cm x 166.7cm, which is nearly a Golden Rectangle. That would make sense, since Dali was intent on combining his religious beliefs (he was a Roman Catholic) with science, and, as we know, the dodecahedron, made entirely of pentagons, is defined by phi. However, most reproductions of the painting are in a ratio of about 1.5, which means some cropping has taken place," Grandpa explained.

The Truncated Icosahedron

"Of all the Platonic Solids, the dodecahedron is the roundest, but still doesn't make a very good ball. But Archimedes, in about 250 B.C., invented what are now known as the Archimedean Solids. These solids are made of two or more regular polygons arranged symmetrically as faces of polyhedra with common vertices, to create a new solid. There are 13 of them, and I encourage you and the Reader to go to Wikipedia to learn more about them.

"One of them is made by starting with an icosahedron, and cutting off its 12 vertices to make 12 pentagon faces. This leaves the 20 faces left as hexagons. Here is what one looks like," said Grandpa.

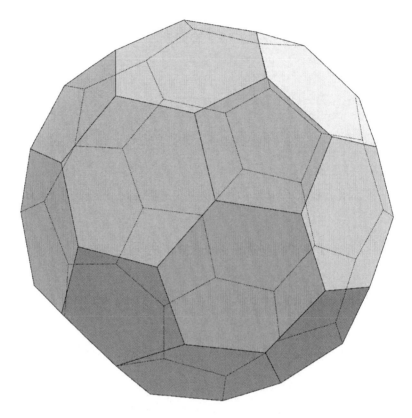

Figure 6.8. The Truncated Icosahedron

"Does this shape look familiar?" Grandpa asked.

"No, I don't think so," said Courtney.

"Maybe it will help if we color the hexagons white and the pentagons black," Grandpa suggested.

Figure 6.9. A Soccer Ball

"A soccer ball!" exclaimed Hunter.

"I've been kicking around a truncated icosahedron!" added Morgan.

"Maybe now you'll have more respect for the ball," commented Courtney.

165

Buckyballs

"Now it turns out there's another interesting place we find truncated icosahedrons," said Grandpa. "This time it's in nature! Up until 1985, it was thought that there were only two basic crystalline forms of carbon; diamond and graphite. But in 1985, a new form was discovered, and it was named fullerene, or buckminsterfullerene.

"It exists in two forms, either a cylinder (called a nanotube) or a ball, or cage, made up of 12 pentagons and 20 hexagons. Does that sound familiar?" asked Grandpa.

"Is it also a soccer ball?" asked Courtney, "Or, I should say, a truncated icosahedron?" She smiled.

"Yep, and here's what it would look like if you could see it. There's a carbon atom at each vertex, and it's called carbon 60, or C_{60}," said Grandpa.

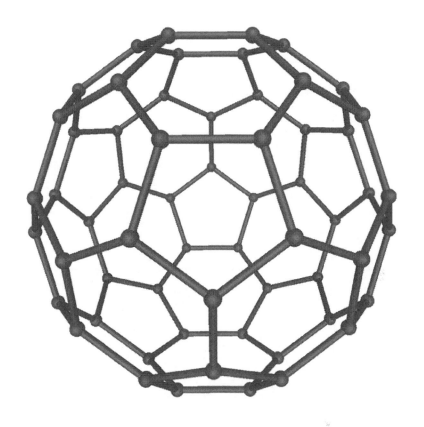

Figure 6.10. A Buckyball

"Yes, that's a soccer ball shape, all right," said Hunter. "But I'll bet it's pretty small."

"It's 220,000,000 times smaller than a soccer ball," replied Grandpa. "So you're not likely to kick one around and know it!

"Fullerene got its name in honor of Buckminster Fuller, who was an American architect who used a similar structure to make his geodesic domes. Those domes have been built for many structures, like homes and radar domes, and even huge ones for the Canadian Olympics and Epcot Center at Disneyworld.

Figure 6.11. Epcot Center at Disney World

"They are very strong for their weight, and can be built using many identical parts, which is very efficient. As you see, the triangles make up hexagons, but the arrangement is not strictly regular. Like dimples on a golf ball, it is very difficult, maybe impossible, to get both uniform coverage and symmetry.

168

"Anyway, let's move on," suggested Grandpa.

From Atoms to Galaxies

"Here's a photo of our galaxy taken from a photographer in some other galaxy," said Grandpa.

Figure 6.12. The Pinwheel Galaxy

"Grandpa, that's silly. We can't have a photo of our own galaxy," Courtney said.

"Well, OK," Grandpa replied, "just checking to see if you were still awake. This is a photo of a galaxy called the Pinwheel Galaxy, and it probably looks a lot like ours. Notice anything about it?"

"Spirals," announced Morgan.

"Yes, I've noticed that in photos of galaxies before," added Hunter.

"I wonder what causes the spirals", said Courtney.

"The typical explanation is that the spirals are brighter because there are more young, brighter stars in the spiral arms. But I have another idea. I think it might be more of a traffic problem," said Grandpa.

Galaxy Traffic

"It's generally accepted that the stars circulate around the center of the galaxy in orbits, and orbits are always elliptical. So let's draw our own galaxy," suggested Grandpa.

"We'll use some computer drawing software for this. I've got Visio on my laptop, so let's use that. Our Reader might have some other graphic software, which is fine. We just need to be able to draw ellipses, and to be able to rotate their axes slightly," said Grandpa.

"I don't get it yet," said Hunter.

"You'll see in a minute," Grandpa replied. "First, let's draw a bunch of ellipses. We'll make a small one, and copy and paste it to get another one, and then drag it's handle to make a larger one, and on and on."

Within just a few minutes, they had a whole bunch of ellipses.

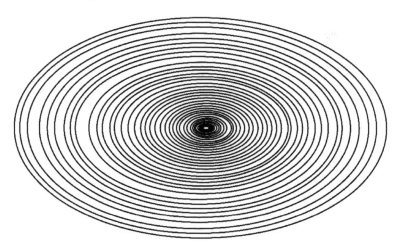

Figure 6.13. Cluster of Ellipses

"OK, now the fun part," said Grandpa, "Let's rotate each ellipse a couple of degrees."

So, taking turns, they clicked on each ellipse and dragged one of its handles to rotate it slightly. They didn't have to do too many to see the pattern start to emerge. When they were finished, they had this beautiful and surprising figure:

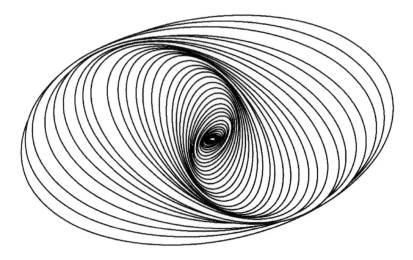

Figure 6.14. Rotated Ellipses

"Wow! That's a surprise," said everyone at once.

"Let's make the lines dotted lines, so we'll have some stars," suggested Grandpa.

So a couple of mouse clicks later, they had this "galaxy".

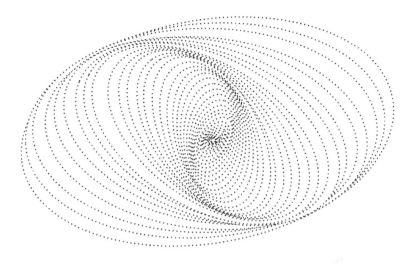

Figure 6.15. Our "Galaxy"

"Wait a minute," said Grandpa, "we've got a bunch of black stars in a white universe. Let's use Paint Shop and make it a negative."

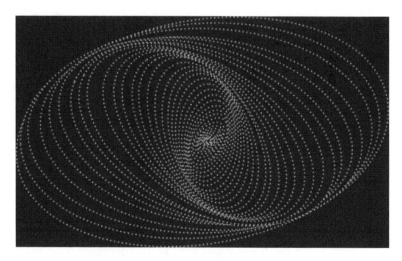

Figure 6.16. Our "Galaxy" Negative

173

"There."

"What's going on here," asked Courtney. "How did we get spirals out of ellipses? And is that what is really happening in space?"

"Maybe," replied Grandpa, "I've never been very satisfied with the explanation that the arms are the only places where new stars are being formed. Maybe there's an explanation, but so far I've not seen a reason why new stars only form in the spiral arms. It seems more reasonable to me that the arms are just the effect of a traffic jam."

"A traffic jam?" asked Hunter.

"Think about traffic on a highway," suggested Grandpa. "Three lanes all running smoothly. Then a road crew shows up to repair a pothole in one of the lanes. It doesn't stop traffic, but it slows it down near the construction zone. Now if you're on a hill looking down on the road, what do you see?"

"The cars get all bunched up," said Morgan. "It's a traffic jam."

"So there are more cars near the construction zone. But are there more cars total?" asked Grandpa.

174

"Oh, I see," said Courtney, "the cars are closer together, but they are leaving as fast as they are arriving. So the bunch-up doesn't move, but the cars are."

"That's right," replied Grandpa. "The density of cars is higher near the slowdown, but the total number of cars is the same. So if the stars in our example are zooming around their orbits, what happens when their orbits intersect, or come closer to each other?"

"That's it," said Hunter, "the density is higher, which is exactly what we see in the diagram. Is that what's happening in space?"

"Well," replied Grandpa, "certainly the arms are brighter than the rest of the galaxy. Maybe it's because there are more stars being formed there, or because their orbits are coming closer to each other so the density is higher, or both. As usual, more knowledge gives us more questions.

A Spiral Aurora

"For example, here's a photo of a spiral aurora borealis. These are rare, but not unheard of. Now we know that the auroras are caused by charged particles from the sun following the earth's magnetic lines inward toward the magnetic poles. And their color is a function of the altitude. But what causes the spiral shape?"

Figure 6.17. A Spiral Aurora Borealis

"Wow. That is definitely spectacular. It certainly gives us another thing to wonder about," said Hunter.

"Yes, and some other time we'll talk about the atmosphere and space and learn more about these things. But now back to numbers!" said Grandpa.

Phi in Art, Architecture, Myths, and Folklore

"Grandpa," Courtney asked, "We saw that Dali's painting probably was in the form of a Golden Rectangle. And of course our own country's flag is decorated with 50 pentagrams. We see Fibonacci numbers in plants, fruits, and flowers. We've seen pentagons in molecules and spirals in sea shells, auroras, and galaxies. Is phi really everywhere?"

"Courtney, when you Google 'golden section', or any of the other terms involving phi, you and the Reader will see many examples of the Golden Rectangle and other figures that contain phi. I think you'll admit that any of us can use the number or the ratio in practically anything we design. So, to me, man's use of phi is not nearly as fascinating as its natural occurrence in the world around us. But it is interesting, and indicates man's interest in phi over the centuries.

"You'll see claims that the Greek Pantheon fits a Golden Rectangle, and it does if you decide where to place the rectangular outline. You'll also see

177

discoveries regarding the ancient pyramids, but lots of those calculations are discredited now that more accurate measurements are made. But there are a lot of 'maybes' and some outright weird ones.

"Phi and the Fibonacci numbers can be found in physiology, even. But to me, I find it hard to be filled with wonder just because we have five fingers on one hand (which is a Fibonacci number). After all, we have a total of ten fingers (which is not) and 20 fingers and toes (which also is not). The human body can be fitted into a Golden Rectangle, but so will lots of things. People point out that on a piano there are eight white keys and five black keys, for a total of 13 notes in an octave on the piano. But there are really 12 notes in an octave, not 13. And phi and the Golden Section, and especially pentagons and pentagraphs (also called pentacles), find their way into religions, cults, and folklore. The reason, of course, is because the appearance in nature and math is so surprising that it is easy to give these symbols some supernatural qualities.

"But the most interesting thing to me is when phi shows up unexpectedly, in nature, math, and physics, and to try to figure out why."

Chapter 7. Solving the Puzzle

"OK, Grandpa," smiled Courtney, "why?"

"I think it is efficiency," replied Grandpa. "One of the main things that nature rewards is efficiency. This shows up in the way seeds are packed into a seed head of a sunflower, the way branches divide, and the way leaves are arranged on a stem so that each leaf gets the most light possible. Remember that in the Fibonacci Series, each number is the sum of the preceding two numbers, and that's the way the growth often happens. A sea shell that shows a spiral construction is a perfect example.

"So nature was using math and geometry in living things long before we discovered it."

Did We Invent Math or Discover It?

"This is a long-standing question that makes you think hard: whether math has been discovered or invented by man," said Grandpa. "What do you think?"

"We discover things that were already there, but we invent new things," offered Courtney.

"Yes, but man invented numbers. Like Fibonacci decided that the Arabic numbers were more useful than the Roman numbers, so that's an invention," countered Morgan.

"I wonder if we would have discovered the Fibonacci series and phi if we were still using Roman numbers and the abacus to calculate things. I hate to think about an irrational number expressed in Roman numerals," said Hunter, "In fact, I can't even see how it could be done!"

"So nature uses phi, along with the geometrical figures it defines, and the series that represents it, and the proportional (Golden) ratio, but we wouldn't have ever known it if we hadn't invented math and geometry," added Courtney.

"If we hadn't invented math and geometry *in a form* that allows us to see it," said Grandpa. "Morgan has correctly pointed out that if we didn't have math in the correct format, we might not have discovered phi."

"So we invented math and discovered phi," concluded Courtney.

"I guess that's a good as we can expect," said Grandpa. "As you study more, and this gets into other fields of study like philosophy, questions like these are fun to explore.

Is God a Mathematician?

"Over the centuries, these questions have intrigued many famous minds. Sir Isaac Newton believed in the Divine Mind that was responsible for these wonders.

"Clifford A. Pickover, a mathematician at IBM, wrote a great book you should read entitled 'The Loom of God.' In it he says 'I do not know if God is a mathematician, but mathematics is the loom upon which God wove the universe... The fact that reality can be described or approximated by *simple* mathematical expressions suggests to me that nature has mathematics at its core'."

"Gee, Grandpa. To think that counting the petals on flowers leads to such universal questions is awesome," said Coutney.

"Yes, nature is full of these kinds of things. We've got a nice long summer coming up, so what do you say we start exploring other interesting subjects later?" asked Grandpa.

"I'm in," replied all three. "See you here by the pool next Saturday!"

The End

Appendix: Calculating Phi, the Magic Number

"OK, let's get started", Grandpa said. "We're going to begin by drawing a line, and then dividing it at a special place along its length. The special place will be so that the proportions of the parts will have a particular relationship to each other. Here's the line:"

"So that we know what parts of the line we are talking about, we'll label some points on the line:"

"We want to divide the line at Point C so that the small part of the line is in the same proportion to the large part as the large part is to the whole line." Grandpa could tell this was a time to stop and let this concept soak in.

"Well," Courtney said, "I can see that if C is put in the middle of the line, the two small parts would be equal, and that wouldn't be proportional to the whole line."

"Yes," Morgan added, "and if C is too far near one end or the other, that won't work either."

"That's correct", Grandpa said, "and in fact there is only one place C can be, and we need to use some algebra to find that point. But don't worry, let's just take it one step at a time."

"First we'll simplify our labeling a little bit by giving the segment CB the length "x", and making the other segment (AC) equal to 1. That way x will be the number we are looking for. Now what's the total line length?"

"X plus one?" Courtney ventured.

"Right on, Cort. So the three pieces of line we are interested in are 1, x, and x+1. And we want these lengths to be proportional to each other. In other words,

1 is to x as x is to x+1."

"Ouch," Morgan groaned.

"Wait a minute," Hunter added, "what if we use real numbers? Two is to four as four is to eight, isn't it?"

"Yes", Grandpa replied, "that is certainly a proportion. But two plus four is six, not eight, so your example doesn't quite fill our need here, does it? So we need a smaller number, and I think you've just shown us that the number we are looking for is less than two, isn't it?"

"What about 1.5 then?" Morgan wondered. "I think we'll need a calculator."

"We can't just sit here trying numbers over and over, can we?" Grandpa suggested. "Here is where we need algebra. We need to make an equation for x and solve it. Then we'll really have the number we want. Are we up for that?"

"I'm taking algebra already", Courtney offered.

"And I'll be into it soon, so I can watch – maybe get a step ahead of Brian." Hunter said.

"I won't look," said Morgan. But we knew that he was going to soak up all he could. Besides, from what I had told him, the best was yet to come.

"OK, Grandpa announced. "Here we go. Here's how we express the ratio (which means fraction, remember?) of the pieces of the line. Recall that we said that 1 is to x as x is to x+1. Expressed algebraically, it looks like this:"

$$\frac{1}{x} = \frac{x}{x+1}$$

"Now to get rid of the fractions, we multiply both sides by x times x+1, and we get this."

$$x + 1 = x^2$$

"To solve this equation for x, we want to rearrange things into a more recognizable form. So we swap sides to get x^2 by itself on the left:"

$$x^2 = x + 1$$

"And then we subtract $x+1$ from both sides to get all the other components on the left, also:"

$$x^2 - x - 1 = 0$$

"Now we can solve for x," Grandpa announced.

"Oh, sure," Morgan said, "Just give me a minute."

"I recognize it." Courtney said, "It's a quadratic equation. We are plotting graphs of those at school. But I'm not sure how to find x."

"There's a famous equation to solve quadratic equations, and I had to memorize it my freshman year in engineering school. And, believe it or not, I still remember it.

"The first thing is to look at the general form of a quadratic equation:"

$$ax^2 + bx + c = 0$$

"And this is why we wanted to get the equation into the format we did, because we need to know what a, b, and c are. So what's the value of "a"?" Grandpa asked.

"There's no "a" in our equation, so it must be zero", Hunter wondered aloud.

"No," Courtney responded, "ax^2 means a times x squared, and if a is zero, ax^2 would vanish. So "a" must be one."

"Right on." Grandpa said, "When the coefficient of a variable is one, it usually gets eliminated. "1x" is just written as "x", but "2x" has to show the "2". Now, what is "b"?"

"It must also be 1", Morgan said. "Because I can't see any other number there."

"Yes, it's one, all right, but also notice that the general equation shows +bx and our equation is –x. How do we change the sign from positive to negative?"

"Multiply by "-1", Courtney said.

"Yes, so "b" must be minus one. How about "c"?" I asked.

"Also minus one." Hunter said.

"Yep. So here are our coefficients:"

$$a = 1$$
$$b = -1$$
$$c = -1$$

"Now the next thing we need to realize that we should expect two solutions to the equation. The reason can be seen pretty easily. What's the solution to this equation?"

$$x^2 = 4$$

"Two!" Hunter announced. "Two squared is four."

"Yes," Grandpa said, "and what is the other answer? Since quadratic equations have two answers, there must be another one."

"Minus two," Courtney offered. "A minus times a minus is plus. Or, as we say in class, two negative numbers multiplied together give a positive answer."

"That's right. We would say that the answer is plus two and minus two (or, to be more exact, positive two and negative two). In math, we write the answer as "plus and minus two:"

$$x = \pm 2$$

"Now we are ready to see the general solution for a quadratic equation:"

$$x = \frac{-b \pm \sqrt{b^2 - 4ac}}{2a}$$

"Don't you just love it?" Grandpa teased. "And the plus and minus sign shows that there are two solutions; one using the plus sign and one using the minus sign."

"Grandpa, did you really remember that?" Morgan wondered.

"Well, I'll have to digress a little here, because of a lesson I learned in college. Freshman engineering students have to take two math courses that form the basis for later higher math. One is algebra, and the other is trigonometry. I had two very different teachers for those two classes. Our algebra teacher collected and graded our homework, and would even point to one of us in class now and then and say "What is the quadratic equation?" for example. We were afraid to say "I don't know", so we learned it, along with whatever else he wanted to teach us.

"On the other hand, our trig class was much more fun. No homework, no spot quizzes, just lecture sprinkled with a lot of fun stories and jokes. Easy class, huh?

"There were other algebra and trig classes with other teachers teaching also, so we engineering students didn't all have the same class, much less the same instructors. But we had a departmental final exam at the end, where all the students had the same test. And do

190

you know what happened? Those of us in my algebra class scored at the top, and those of us in our trig class, including me, scored at the bottom. We had obviously learned algebra, but did very poorly in trig.

"Well, the trig teacher got fired, but that didn't put trig in our heads. And how we suffered later! Calculus, and especially advanced calculus was many times more difficult than it needed to be for those of us with a poor trigonometry background. And what a contrast we could see between those two teachers.

"Anyhow, the lesson is this: even though a teacher might be easy on you, make sure you are learning the material. Learning the stuff is much more important than just getting an easy grade. Got it?"

"Yes, Grandpa, the knowledge is much more important than the grade if you're going to keep going, right?" Hunter commented.

"Right. And now let's solve that equation. To summarize, we have

$$x^2 - x - 1 = 0,$$

$$a = 1$$
$$b = -1$$
$$c = -1$$

And

$$x = \frac{-b \pm \sqrt{b^2 - 4ac}}{2a}$$

"The –b is –(-1), right?" Grandpa said, to get things started.

"Yes, which is +1," Courtney offered. "And b² is -1 times -1, which is also +1."

Hunter piped up "Let me do the -4ac! Since c is -1 and a is +1, a times c is -1. And -1 times 4 is -4, right?"

"Good, Hunter. Now in the equations we have -4ac, which is the negative of the product of 4ac. So if 4ac is equal to -4, what is -4ac?"

"Plus 4" chimed in Courtney.

"Right again, Court." Grandpa said, "Now there's only one expression left in the formula, and we'll give that to Morgan to solve. Morgan?"

"You mean the 2a, Grandpa?" Morgan asked.
"Well, a is +1, so I suppose two times one is two.
Everybody knows that."

"Yes, Morgan, I'm sure everybody does.
Anyhow, now we are ready to put the numbers into the
equation:"

$$x = \frac{1 \pm \sqrt{1+4}}{2}$$

"And when we add the one and four, we get"

$$x = \frac{1 \pm \sqrt{5}}{2}$$

"Now if we are going to turn this into our magic
number, we are going to need a calculator. Hunter,
there's one right over there in the top drawer. Make
sure it can do square roots, though."

"I've got it, Grandpa. Should I calculate the
square root of five?"

"Yes." Grandpa replied, "And I think you are
going to get a lot of digits in the number."

"Ta-da! The answer is 2.23606798." Hunter
announced.

"Yes," Grandpa said, "almost."

"What do you mean, Grandpa?" Courtney asked. "The answer is right there on the screen."

"That's true," Grandpa replied, "as far as it goes. This calculator can only show us nine digits. But the square root of 5, like many other numbers, is infinitely long, and can never be expressed exactly. It's called "irrational", meaning that it can never be expressed exactly as a numerical ratio, or fraction."

"There are lots of irrational numbers?" Morgan wondered.

"Yes," I replied, "like the square root of three, or two, or pi. You know what pi is, right?"

"Yes," Courtney replied, "it's in all the circle equations."

"True. Basically, it's the ratio of the circumference of a circle to its diameter. Notice that just because it's an irrational number doesn't mean it's not real. We can measure the diameter and circumference of the wheels on our bicycles, can't we? And we can measure them as exactly as we can, and when we divide them we will get pi, and it will be an irrational number. And our magic number is also going to be irrational, because we can already see that the square root of five is there. So let's go ahead and calculate it. Then the fun begins."

"OK," Courtney said, "one plus the square root of five is 3.23606798, and when we divide it by two, we'll have the answer!"

"I can't wait," Morgan said, "I'm shaking all over."

"Get back in your cage, Morgan." Hunter said. "Let's see, we need to divide 3.23606798 by two. The answer is....."

After a suitable drum roll, Hunter laid the number on us.

"1.61803399"

"Right on," Grandpa said, "and to show that it's an irrational number, meaning that there are more digits we can't see, we usually put three periods behind it, like this:

1.61803399...

"And that, ladies and gentlemen, is defined as ϕ.

Some other time we will talk about other ways to derive ϕ, including its relationship to two other famous irrational numbers, π and e.

"Now back to the text. We are going to explore both geometry and nature, and you'll soon see why some of the past's great thinkers have called this 'God's Number'".

About the Author

Mr. Choisser is an electronic engineer who has written and edited many articles, papers, and publications over the years. He has started several high-tech companies, and has several patents and awards for his technical achievements. He particularly enjoys educating and motivating others, whether they are associates, friends, or family. As his children grew up, he particularly enjoyed cooking, singing, and telling stories with them.

His hobbies include cooking, golfing, sailing, gardening, and writing. Most of his current publications can be found on Amazon, by selecting "books" and searching for "Choisser."

He can be contacted through Facebook and LinkedIn.

Made in the USA
San Bernardino, CA
04 December 2019